# CONCILIUM

CONCILIUM                    2001/1

# GOD: EXPERIENCE AND MYSTERY

Edited by

Werner Jeanrond and Christoph Theobald

with Seán Freyne and Giuseppe Ruggieri

SCM Press · London

Published by SCM Press, 9–17 St Albans Place, London N1

ISBN: 0 334 03062 5

Printed by Biddles Ltd, Guildford and King's Lynn

*Concilium* Published February, April, June, October,
December

# Contents

III.  Divine Revelation, Hermeneutics and Truth

# Introduction

WERNER G. JEANROND AND CHRISTOPH THEOBALD

Since the 1970s the understanding of God in the various contexts of Christianity has been undergoing some significant changes. Political theology, radical theology, liberation theology, feminist theology, ecological theology, gay and lesbian theology, contextual theology, post-colonial theology, and other emancipatory theological projects have claimed new insights into God's mysterious presence in our world. As a result, images and concepts of God have been changing, traditional attributes of God (e.g. omnipotence, inability to suffer, aseity) have been questioned, and the trinitarian understanding of God has been reinterpreted in a number of different ways. During the same period, efforts have been made to retrieve some aspects of apophatic and mystical theologies from the past now in critical correlation to postmodern philosophical thinking and contemporary religious experience. Moreover, experiences of both the inter-religious encounter and the ongoing inter-religious dialogue have contributed to a different understanding and to changing images of God's presence in our world and promoted the challenge to traditional modes of referring to God in more or less exclusivist and static terms.

These new departures in reflecting upon God have also led to a renewed attention to the biblical understanding of God. Traditional biblical theologies have been questioned and new and more critical biblical theologies have been called for. Also major texts of the Christian traditions are being re-examined in terms of possible proposals for alternative ways of experiencing God and of thinking about the divine mystery.

This issue of *Concilium* would like to explore some of these recent ways of rethinking the Christian experiences of God in terms of their new quality, their methodological profile and their potential for renewing the Christain faith at the beginning of the new millennium. In a first move, a few recent experiences of God are described and assessed in order to grasp some among the changing perceptions of the divine mystery between, on the one hand, increasing globalization and, on the other hand, increasing regionalization. In a second move, Christian traditions of thinking about God, biblical and postbiblical, will be reinterpreted in view of the contemporary changes, and vice versa. Finally, the concept of revelation as well as the truth status of these recent experiences of God are examined and the hermeneutical question asked how the Christian understanding of God may best be protected against immediatist and fundamentalist claims, on the one hand, and against traditionalist and relativist claims, on the other hand.

The editors wish to thank Seán Freyne and Giuseppe Ruggieri for valuable assistance during the preparation of this issue.

# I. Recent Experiences of God in Different Contexts of Church and Society

# The Experience of God in Christian Liturgy

### DAVID N. POWER

Of late, a number of liturgical theologians have argued that there needs to be a place for liturgy in foundational theology.[1] This is because liturgy is considered the privileged place in the life of the church for the mediation of grace to believers and for the expression in living and lively form of the church's faith and communion with God. In it, human and Christian experience is given shape and direction and faith in Christ and in God is given its most fundamental expression, according to the axiom which allies the law of belief with the law of prayer. Not only then is there an experience of God in liturgical action but the critical interpretation of liturgical forms and celebration enables an understanding of the experience of grace and communion with God throughout the entire course of Christian life and human history.

There are different ways of explaining this. For an Orthodox theologian such as Vladimir Lossky,[2] for example, it is only in and through liturgy and the associated display of icons that the life of God is mediated. What is there given is to flow over into the whole of life which is to be lived as a way into deeper communion with the divine Trinity through a process of deification. Hence one kind of theology, called cataphatic, is the elucidation of what is given expression, and the final theology is apophatic communion with God, the goal and purpose of liturgy and of explicative theology. Taking a somewhat different approach to an explanation of liturgy, today many Catholic scholars have been inspired by the insights of Karl Rahner into the connection between liturgy and the fuller human experience of God in all of life. From this perspective, sacramental mediation gives shape, form, development and fullness to the experience of God found in any human encounter with creation and throughout life.[3] In either case, the experience of God for the Christian is intimately tied with liturgy and it is through an analysis of liturgical expression that the nature of this experience may be probed. However, it is the avenue of liturgical expression's relation to the wider experience of human existence that seems the more fruitful for an understanding today of the experience which believers have of God in and through liturgy.

## I. Liturgical mediation

A good understanding of the way in which liturgical celebration mediates the experience of the divine derives from the insight that it is both an interpretation of the salvation offered by God through Christ and the Spirit and an interpretation of human life as lived in its entirety as a graced communion. On the one hand liturgy is the expression and celebration of the church as it gives form to its belief in the gospel and the mediation of grace so that it can rightly be dubbed the church's activity and self-expression. On the other hand, what is offered through a liturgy that belongs in a long tradition remains what precedes any such expression. It is what is passed on through a living tradition from the time of the community of first believers who were chosen to be the witnesses of the teaching, life, death and resurrection of Jesus Christ. Of language in general or of the language of any particular culture, it is said from one point of view that people express themselves, or speak, a language. From another point of view, it is said that they are spoken by the language inasmuch as it is something passed on to them from preceding generations, as well as a medium through which other earthly and cosmic realities address them. This insight can be evoked in understanding the role of liturgy in the life of Christian believers. Though there is a sense in which the church through its liturgy grasps and enunciates the experience of God given in Christ, there is a more fundamental sense in which what is spoken in tradition in God's name grasps the church and enfolds it in a mystery which is beyond its comprehension. The very language in which she expresses herself, precedes her. No constitution of a liturgical rite and no liturgical reform or revision, whether it be Orthodox, Protestant or Catholic, can be done independently of the language and form in which the gospel and the offer of grace have been handed on from the beginning. Fidelity to God's advent into history means that even as liturgical expression necessarily changes, the church continually traces it back as it were to its originating expressions, recognizing this as God's own gift and advent.

It is not a matter, however, of an original and unadulterated sacramental form being stamped on all peoples and cultures. Rather as the liturgical words, signs and actions weave their way into historical reality, cultural expression and the common life of any era or place, liturgical action is a constantly renewed event of the Word and Spirit of God. In virtue of the original event of the cross, Christ continues to find a place in human reality, in ever fresh forms of proclamation, praise and liturgical sign. Woven into life, history and culture through liturgy, God's saving action is not an other-worldly offer of grace that calls on Christians to transcend this world and enter into some sacred space of existence, but it is a this-worldly event that relates to the particular cultural, social and historical being of peoples. The sacred or the holy of the experience of God is an indwelling in human life through the medium of human artifacts that recall and represent the event of God's saving action through creation, covenant and the mysteries of Christ's flesh.

## *1. Religious metaphors*

In the course of the centuries, and in various ways from locality to locality, this presence of God, in Christ and in the memorial of Christ, has been portrayed in terms that draw on a variety of biblical and religious metaphors. Sometimes it has been proclaimed and celebrated as the mystery of Christ's expiating and redeeming sacrifice. In other liturgical families or periods, the prevailing metaphor has been that of entry into Christ's own passage to the Father by passage through the sacraments. In our present time, as pointed out by Pope John Paul II in his encyclical *Fides et Ratio*, the imagery of the self-emptying or *kenosis* of the Word, or indeed of God's own loving self-gift, is often evoked to speak of the mystery of the divine entry into the pain and suffering of the world in order to redeem and reconcile a humanity pulled apart by pain and even out of harmony with the earth on which it dwells. In this very diversity of ways of letting tradition speak and of naming the advent and presence of God in the world and in the church, there is a diversity in how this is experienced.

The interpretation, therefore, of how liturgical expression mediates and shapes the experience of God must be both analytical and critical. It has to decipher the forms of liturgical expression to see how they name God, Christ, Spirit, church and grace by the constant memory of Christ and by fidelity to what has been passed on, not only in substance but in privileged forms. But it also has to be critical of the ways in which church communities relate this to the particular social, historical and cultural experiences of their own existence, since in this endeavour not only is the necessary particular-ization realized but some elements that are alien to divine life may also be inserted.

In an analysis of the experience of God given through liturgy, a starting-point is to take note of how it engages all the senses, engages the imagination and engages the very memory by which human persons and societies relate their being and activity to past, present and future. The core characteristics of sacramental expression and of memorial praise is a good place to begin in order to see what is at the heart of the encounter of God with his people.

## 2. Sacramental signs

The key sacramental signs of bread, wine, oil and water dig deeply into our humanity as persons and as communities, living in every fibre of our being through a communion with the earth which we inhabit and the cosmos which surrounds us. While it is rightly said that these things are fruit of the earth and work of human hands, they need to be seen fully in all that they evoke of humanity's oneness with earthly and cosmic reality and of the need of being in communion with others for them to be produced and shared for the common good. At the same time, they evoke the agony of life when due to dependence on earthly and cosmic forces these goods are lacking, or when because of the opposition and animosity of human beings to one another they are not shared. It is into the life signified so widely and deeply in these goods that God's grace enters and it is in this life that the transforming power of the Word and the Spirit are at work through the medium of liturgical action.

## 3. Sacramental words

When our being is thus brought to expression and the place for the entry of God's grace opened up, being in Christ is given form through the proclamation of the Word and through the prayer in which worshippers are united in his name and in his Spirit. That praise, thanksgiving and intercession are the key ways of addressing God expresses our relation to him as creator, covenant maker and redeemer. We exist and live through the open and willing reception of what is offered to us through creation, covenant and redemption from sin, as Word and Spirit take form within us through this means in the here and now of our existence. Proclamation indeed precedes prayer but it is through prayer that the realities are assimilated into existence, God always acting in and through our own human articulation.

## II. Keeping memorial

When the church is invited to keep memorial of Jesus Christ, to remember him at the heart of every liturgical action, she is by the same token invited to engage with human memories and with her perspective on the relation between past, present and future. This was the fine point of the exhortation to the purification of memories in the Jubilee year of 2000. God encounters us also in the purification of memories, not only because he offers pardon to what the church now acknowledges as fault but also because in the recognition of how this fault has distorted the memory of Christ in the past. The texts and rites that come from the past speak in new ways, once they are freed from the distorting power of sinfulness and misconception, or from the historically limited cultural, social and institutional forms of life to which they were bound.

Among the things for which the pardon of the Jubilee is sought is the neglect of the histories and the cultures of peoples who were evangelized, especially through the evangelization which took place on the Latin American, African and Asian continents.[4] Any recognition of divine action and presence in these histories and through these cultural forms was not only neglected but indeed generally scorned. This cannot be redressed simply by now allowing some transposition of a Latin liturgy into the language and cultural expressions of these peoples. The purification of memories has to occur within the liturgy in two ways. First the memory of the church's acts of imposition needs to be given a place, as has occurred in different churches, beginning in Rome, in the Jubilee year when pardon was asked in a liturgical setting for past offenses. However, it has to be given place even more importantly as peoples take on the responsibility of evoking their own memories in the face of God and his Christ so that what has been suppressed may be remembered and praised and made the very locus of the memorial of Christ's revelation, death and resurrection. In other words, the experience of God is now offered to peoples through an action of keeping memorial that incorporates what is required for the purification of memories. This is an important part of the actuality of the experience of God in the liturgy, which occurs in virtue of the memory of Christ, in virtue of the signs that evoke all human life on earth, and in virtue of the healing of memories that is empowered through the inspiring role of the Spirit who teaches the church what she ought to pray.

Of course in order to be active and integrated into human experience as lived in the concrete, all liturgical expression is necessarily limited. The memory of Christ engages with people's own memories and this is the condition for a cultural rooting of gospel and sacrament. This is both the wonder and mystery of divine experience. It is always found in life's particularities but by that same token it has to be open to conversation and exchange with other expressions, and finally open in doxology to the mystery that lies beyond us but into which we are nonetheless invited. On the one hand, the Word made flesh takes form anew through its convergence with the memories of peoples and through its proclamation and prayer expression in the language, idiom and rites of diverse peoples. On the other hand, the prayer of doxology has a central role to play in liturgical action, to remind communities that even as the Word comes to them, through the action of the Spirit, finally they are drawn into the eternal and abiding mystery of God which surpasses all expression.

## Notes

1. See A. Grillo, 'L'esperienza rituale come "dato" della teologia fondamentale: ermeneutica di una rimozione e prospettive teoriche di reintegrazione'" in *Liturgia e incarnazione*, a cura di Aldo Natale Terrin, Padua: Edizioni Messagero 1997, pp.167–284.
2. See Vladimir Lossky, *Essai sur la théologie mystique de l'église d'Orient*, Paris: Aubier 1944. Translated into English as *The Mystical Theology of the Eastern Church*, London: James Clark 1957.
3. Succinctly presented in the chapter on sacramental life in *Grundkurs des Glaubens: Einführung in den Begriff des Christentums*, Freiburg im Breisgau: Herder 1976. Translated into English as *Foundations of Christian Faith*, New York: The Seabury Press 1978, pp.411–430.
4. See the document of the International Theological Commission, *Memory and Reconciliation*, note 19.

# A Passion for Life and Justice: Gender and the Experience of God

How *is* God discerned anew in history? Where has God disappeared amidst the apparent victory of sceptical secularism? *Hidden*, in a *Cloud of Un-knowing*, replies the mystic. *Vanished*, like the Cheshire Cat, replies the cynic, perhaps leaving a only cosmic grin behind! *Collapsed*, like Alice in Wonderland's pack of cards, says the postmodern philosopher, because 'he' was ever nothing but a human construct. 'He' *may* have disappeared temporarily, admits the anxious theologian, but *surely* there are footprints of this disappearing God? Yet, in contrast with this anxiety, arising from the families of global feminist theologies vibrant images of the Divine, both ancient and new, are now appearing.[1]

## I. The journey from 'God the Father'

> She say, my first step from the old white man was trees. Then air. Then birds. Then other people. But one day when I was sitting quiet, like a motherless child, which I was, it come to me: that feeling of being part of everything, not separate at all. I knew that if I cut a tree, my arm would bleed.[2]

Alice Walker's quotation encapsulates the urgency felt by feminist theologians to move beyond the patriarchal, distant, controlling, white, male image of God. Although they are joined in this by many contemporary theologians,[3] who argue that this God-figure was always a caricature, yet few of these actually join the project of deconstructing a patriarchal society for which this God-figure acted as preserver and sanctioner.

Much of the thinking of Western feminist theologians as well as that of women of colour, and women struggling for global justice was sparked off by the critique of Mary Daly's book *Beyond God the Father*.[4] This book, a catalyst in articulating resistance to the powerful grip that patriarchy held on culture's dominant symbols and images, illuminated the way that the traditional symbolism of *God the Father* functioned to exclude women from positions of authority and to exclude female imagery from symbolizing the Divine.[5] It reinforced the supposition that maleness is normative for humanity: 'he is the subject, she is the other'.[6] In Christian theological terms, it meant not only that women had no role models for the full becoming of women, calling into question the whole significance of the Mystery of the Incarnation for women,[7] but also that exclusively male images for God (Father, Judge, Lord, King, Warrior) were embodied and legitimized by the power structures of patriarchal or *kyriarchal*[8] society.

The cultural effects of this imagery may well often be hidden, but in a macho society, where violence prevails on a public level, it can be glaringly evident. In countries under oppressive military dictatorships, masculinity is linked with military and sexual violence: but, husbands abusing wives and children is a global phenomenon: in fact, the existence of violent and abusive behaviour of fathers towards their children highlights the desperate need for a *redeemed father* image for God, since the human analogue seems to be failing so badly. In a sensitive article, the theologian Janet Martin Soskice asked if a feminist can in fact call God 'Father'.[9] Perhaps, what Jesus was doing through his own name for God, a term of endearment, 'Abba', was indeed to rid 'Father' of patriarchal, controlling, distant and violent overtones. So, along with reclaiming a 'good' father image, theology now questions whether, in fact, the 'Father' God functioning to exclude the full becoming of women, far from being the authentic God of Judaism or Christianity, is not a distortion, a projection or caricature in societies justifying male dominance and power.

## II. Imagining a new symbolic world

Breaking out of what seemed like a strait-jacket in thinking about God, poets, artists, musicians have led the way. Many women – and men – confessed to being starved of nourishment and experience of the Divine by the poverty and one-sidedness of the language for God. Once the floodgates were opened, a richness of imagery, an unceasing creativity has blazed a trail for an extraordinary renewal of Christian religious experience.

First, a whole range of images and symbols counterbalances the maleness of God with God imagined as female. These include Meinrad Craighead's paintings of God-as-Mother giving birth to the world,[10] attempts to image an inclusive Trinity (God as creator, pain-bearer and lover), and Janet Morley's beautiful re-writing of the psalms with God as mother and lover at their heart:

> I will praise God, my Beloved,
> for she is altogether lovely.
> Her presence satisfies my soul;
> she fills my senses to overflowing
> so that I cannot speak. [11]

The hymn-writer Brian Wren brings together of many of these images:

> Who is She, neither male nor female, maker of all things,
> only glimpsed or hinted, source of life and gender?
> She is God,
> mother, sister, lover: in her love we wake, move, grow,
> are daunted, triumph and surrender. [12]

## III. If not our Father, our Mother?

The reclaiming of the image of God as Mother spans all the religions as well as inspiring ecological, earth-based spiritualities. Within Christian theological tradition it is a minor strand, the idea of Christ as our Mother being found in Anselm and Julian of Norwich. There is now enormous enthusiasm in many circles in discovering the ancient goddess traditions, as empowerment for the full becoming of women. Many women have left traditional Christianity 'to follow the goddess'. How should Christian theology respond?

The Goddess – often Goddess means the universal earth Mother figure, common to most ancient religions – represents the interconnectedness of all things, holding human beings in interdependent relation with each other and with the earth. According to Carol Christ, the Goddess appears in a multiplicity of forms,[13] and in the three phases of being woman, as maiden, mother and wise woman (crone). To embrace the Goddess as the living web of life, she writes, enables us to alter our views on death, life after death and tragedy. We will no longer hold on to immortality as our birthright because the Goddess has taught us how to respect the seasons of giving birth and dying.

What can be learnt from the Goddess movements is, first, the emphasis on the *healing of wounded bodies*. Women – and any person – who have suffered oppression under patriarchy are brought into a completely new space where the female body and sexuality are valued. It is impossible to overestimate the healing value of rituals focussing on reverencing female bodies which religious traditions have vilified and despised at worst, and controlled and tolerated at best. Secondly, from the care and attention given to all aspects of nature, her rhythms, seasonal variety and diversity of the creatures, there arises an ethic of responsibility for creation manifested by, for example, vegetarianism and care for animals, and the protection and planting of trees. Thirdly, the centrality of female sacred images of the Divine compensates for their lack within Christianity. Lastly, calling the earth and nature 'our mother' makes connections with earth-based spiritualities of indigenous peoples and re-connects with the material base of all living and loving – but without falling into making of nature a divine principle or forgetting that the Mystery of Life we call God/God/ess is always named symbolically and metaphorically. Naming God as she, or Goddess, has been described as a new epiphany of the sacred, a naming which ushers in a new revelation.[14] And the test of metaphors for God is not only their correspondence with tradition, but their success or failure in inspiring new and juster modes of living.

## IV. God, our passion for justice

The struggle for justice has become the unique source in feminist theology for images of God, from diverse contexts. This is one of the key contrasts with traditional theology, namely that feminist theology is not primarily concerned with concepts of God, or in constructing a new systematic theology, but in social change and the transformation of society. The most powerful images emerge from this struggle itself.

The American theologian, Carter Heyward, is inspired by the image of God as passion for relation, or passion for justice, or power in relation. This God is the source of justice, resource for justice, maker of justice and justice herself. God created out of a yearning for relation and mutuality. Secondly, God is revealed through power-in-relation or relational power – in the actual process of redemption and transformation. Divine relational power is successful: God is 'the power that drives to justice and makes it. Makes the sun blaze, the rivers roar, the fires rage. And the revolution is won again.'[15]

This relational power is passionate, spontaneous, raw and unpredictable. Heyward depicts it as crucial in the ministry of Jesus, the embodiment of

God's power-in-relation. This redeeming power of God, which is so often intertwined by feminist theologians with God's creativity, as *the broken web* out of which the reborn world will emerge, embodied in the ministry of Jesus, is embodied again and again by Christic communities of discipleship. 'Relational power' is part of feminist theology's re-imagining of God's power as alternative to the patriarchal power of the 'God of power and might'. It is the power of sensitivity, of compassion, of empathy, of affiliation and bonding.[16] God as source of power-in-relation, is also linked with the idea of *power as erotic energy*.[17] The eros of God, the power which brings healing and wholeness is seen as the 'creating, enlarging and sustaining of relations'.[18] It is 'the power which, at its deepest roots, understands joy and refuses injustice', and is the healing, whole-making power of God.

Finally, within this relational imagery, the transcendence of God is seen as the *power of crossing over*, using the imagery of the bridge:

> To transcend means, literally, to cross over. To bridge. To make connections. To burst free of particular locations. A truly transcendent God knows the bounds of no human life or religion . . .[19]

In *latina* and *mujerista* contexts,[20] God is experienced as fullness of life. Faith in this God of Life is a starting point: discovering God in the faces of the suffering and oppressed led to the belief that 'faith in God means a commitment to transform this situation'.[21] So, the God of fullness of life becomes the God of the transformation of society. The meanings of 'fullness of life' in Latin-American women's experience are not reducible to political utility, but bring increased hope in community, hope for the healed relationship of women and men, an end to *machismo* – and a future for their children. These are the visions of flourishing, the content of faith in the God of life and transformation. But this God of Life is also experienced as a relational God: there is a specific appeal here to women's experiences of motherhood. Thus, according to Ana Maria Tepedino, women experience God 'in their own manner, as the One who really protects the weak and is the defender of those who have less life'. She believes, as does Peruvian Consuela del Prado, that since women carry children in their wombs, they experience God differently, in a 'relational' manner, that 'goes beyond conceptual coldness'. Her experience of life embraces 'strength and tenderness, happiness and tears, intuition and reason'.[22] This imaging of God as relational, life-affirming and present is expressed powerfully by Elsa Tamez in terms of the God of the oppressed, and, specifically including women as both poor and oppressed. But her understanding of oppression goes deeper than political repression: as well as economic oppression (the sin of idolatry), it includes the humiliated bodies of women and men, and the damage to self-esteem, to the inmost dignity of being a person, and includes the lowest level of dehumanization.[23] God's active presence, praxis of justice and availability to all persons are aspects of the way Tamez sees God's embodiment in society. And knowing this God means acting for justice.

That this God of justice is not external to women, but working in and through people of faith, is also an aspect of *mujerista* theology, in the theology of Ada Maria Isasi-Diaz. The content of the images of God expressed by many Hispanic women is that of presence and nearness, at the same time linked with loyalty to their faith community, in a way that is almost mystical. God is also seen here as acting for justice. God acts through our passion for just relation, in our commitment to *God's* passion for justice, and in the depths of God's nearness to us in heart and soul. But God also acts through silence:

> . . . without the silence of God we can't become men and women . . . God remains silent so that men and women may speak, protest, and struggle. God remains silent so that we may become really ourselves. When God is silent and men and women cry, God cries in solidarity with them, but God does not intervene, God waits for the shouts of protest. Then God begins to speak again, but in dialogue with us.[24]

This silence of God, is sometimes connected with the mystical Dark Night of the Soul.[25] In this context of God as our passion for just and right relation, I link God's silence, God's *kenosis*, with God's compassion and God's suffering with us.

## V. The compassionate and suffering God[26]

The conviction that 'God weeps with our pain' is a vital part of feminist re-imaging.[27] At root, faith in a God who suffers with us does not so much emerge from a philosophical rejection of the impassible, omnipotent and self-sufficient God, but from the experience of affliction,[28] and of the presence of God within this affliction. But how do we dare to use this suffering as a powerful image of God's own suffering? Although the references to God as mother and midwife to the birth of the new Israel are scarce, yet they speak powerfully to the pain of women. The fact that Jesus, about to suffer, compared the pain he would undergo and the subsequent joy, to the travail of women in childbirth (John 14 ) is a sign of the empathy of Jesus, and that this suffering can be creative for the birthing of the kingdom (or *kin-dom*).[29]

Women from a wide diversity of contexts seem to sense that God is not ashamed to share our pain. Indeed, there is an ancient (if minor) tradition that in martyrdom, in witness to the kingdom, the believer is united with Jesus, the embodiment of God.[30] Contemporary images continue to depict Christ in the form of a woman, in the anguish of giving birth to the new creation.[31] These, one might object, show the suffering love of Christ. But Christian faith trusts that Jesus revealed how God *is*. The passionate love of God for the full humanity of the most marginalized of groups means that God identifies with our pain. But *because God is God, it means that suffering is not all that God does.* God's compassion being poured out ceaselessly is a source of strength for *suffering women*.

## VI. God as Wisdom, Sophia, Hokmah

Many of these strands coalesce in the imaging of God as Sophia, Wisdom. I draw together some of the strands of this discourse to illustrate the richness emerging from the gendered experience of God of contemporary feminist theology.

Sophia, a scriptural figure, is creative energy with God at the dawn of creation (Prov.7; Eccles. 24.3–5). She is teacher (Prov. 8.1–11). Sometimes she is both teacher and what is taught (Prov. 4.5,8). She can be lover, mother and teacher all at the same time (Eccles. 4.11–16). She has an organic link with creation, imaged as tree and plant (Eccles. 24.12–19).[32] Sophia dwells in Israel, and celebrates festive liturgies in the temple. In fact, making people friends of God is characteristic of the activity of Sophia.[33] Secondly, mythologically Sophia is linked with wisdom goddess figures of other ancient Near Eastern cultures – and indeed, the question as to why Sophia became lost from Christian tradition is a fascinating one.[34] The third strand is the way that Sophia as goddess functions as an empowering figure in women's spiritual journey – and I alluded to this in the work of Carol Christ.

Fourthly, the Sophia figure has inspired many feminist liturgies – even provoking negative reactions, largely because of the fear of paganism.[35] But the fifth strand shows how deeply the Sophia image is embedded in Christian theology through, for example, the work of Bulgakov, Florensky and Soloviev. Through Sophia another face of the embodiment of God is offered, another manifestation of God's vulnerability in the world – the female, but not only the female, as the vulnerable face of God – and a manifestation of how tragedy is caught up into God.

Fifthly, I evoked the figure of Sophia as a myth of 'connected living' – non-dualist, ecological, justice-centred and relational.[36] This opposes the *logos* myth – competitive, materialistic, success-oriented and individualistic. Sophia is also evoked as a metaphor for an ecological theology.[37] The last strand is the way feminist theology increasingly integrates Sophia themes within Christian doctrines: God is God as Spirit-Sophia, the mobile, pure, people-loving Spirit who pervades every wretched corner, wailing at the waste, releasing power that enables fresh starts. Her energy quickens the earth to life, her beauty shines in the stars, her strength breaks forth in every fragment of shalom and renewal that transpires in arenas of violence and meaninglessness . . . Sophia-God dwells in the world at its centre and at its edges, an active vitality crying out in labour, birthing the new creation.[38] In the figure of Spirit-Sophia, God-Sophia, feminist theology offers a prophetic challenge to culture's idolatry of power and money. God-Sophia draws on the wisdom of the poor, recalls us to ancient wisdom coming from the earth and embodied existence, to forgotten wisdom cosmologies, and to the hunger and yearning for justice that cannot be quenched. She is the woman hidden in the wilderness of patriarchy for so many centuries (see Rev. 12) but now awakened, emerging, summoning us to deeper epiphanies of the Divine.

## Notes

1. Some of these reflections are developed in my book *Introducing Feminist Images of the Divine*, Sheffield: Sheffield Academic Press 2001.
2. Alice Walker, *The Color Purple*, London: The Women's Press 1983, p.103.
3. See Rowan Williams, *On Christian Theology*, Oxford: Blackwell 2000, p.121.
4. Mary Daly, *Beyond God the Father*, London: The Women's Press 1973.
5. See Rosemary Radford Ruether, *Sexism and God-Talk*, Boston: Beacon Press and London: SCM Press 1983.
6. Simone de Beauvoir, *The Second Sex*, Harmondsworth: Penguin 1973, p.16.
7. This would eventually be thematized in a powerful way by Luce Irigaray, 'Femmes Divines' (1985), reprinted in *Sexes et Parentés*, Paris: Editions de Minuit 1987, pp.69–85. It is also the spur to the project of Grace Jantzen in developing a fully-fledged feminist philosophy of religion in *Becoming Divine:*

*Towards a Feminist Philosophy of Religion*, Manchester: Manchester University Press 1998.

8. The Word *kyriarchy* was coined by Elisabeth Schüssler Fiorenza, and means the 'rule of the Lord', thus comprehending in one word the oppression of gender, race and class.

9. Janet Martin Soskice, 'Can a *Feminist Call God "Father"?'* in Teresa Elwes (ed), *Women's Voices: Essays in Contemporary Feminist Theology*, London: Marshall Pickering 1992, pp.15–30.

10. *Meinrad Craighead, The Mother's Songs*, Mahwahm NJ: Paulist Press 1986.

11. Janet Morley, *All Desires Known*, London: MOW and WIT 1988, p.50.

12. Brian Wren, *What Language Shall I Borrow?*, New York: Crossroad and London: SCM Press 1989, pp.141–42.

13. Carol Christ, *Rebirth of the Goddess: Finding Meaning in Feminist Spirituality*, New York: Addison-Wesley 1997.

14. Nelle Morton, *The Journey is Home*, Boston: Beacon Press 1986.

15. Carter Heyward, *The Redemption of God: A Theology of Mutuality*, Washington: University of America Press 1982, p.162.

16. Mary Grey, *Redeeming the Dream: Christianity, Feminism and Redemption*, London: SPCK 1989, pp.103–4.

17. Carter Heyward, *Touching our Strength; The Erotic as Power and Love of God*, San Francisco: Harper and Row 1989.

18. Audre Lorde, *Sister Outsider: Essays and Speeches*, Trumansburg, NY: Crossing Press 1984.

19. Carter Heyward, *Our Passion for Justice*, New York: Pilgrim Press 1984, p.245.

20. *Latina* is the theology of Latin American women; *mujerista* is the theology of Hispanic women mainly in the US, but with links elsewhere.

21. María Pilar Aquino, *Our Cry for Life: Feminist Theology from Latin America*, Maryknoll: Orbis 1993, p.32.

22. Tepedino and Prado in Linda Moody (ed), *Women Encounter God: Theology across the Boundaries of Difference*, Maryknoll: Orbis 1996, pp.63–64.

23. Elsa Tamez, *Bible of the Oppressed*, Maryknoll: Orbis 1982, p.25

24. Elsa Tamez, 'Letter to Job' in Virginia Fabella and Sergio Torres (eds), *Doing Theology in a Divided World*, Maryknoll: Orbis 1985, p.175

25. Mary Grey, *Redeeming the Dream* and *Beyond the Dark Night – A Way Forward for the Church?*, London: Cassell 1997.

26. Since the publication of Jürgen Moltmann's classic, *The Crucified God*, New York: Harper and London: SCM Press 1974, there has been a well-established genre. See Marc Steen, 'The Theme of the Suffering God' in Lambrecht and Collins (eds), *God and Human Suffering*, Leuven: Peters 1989, pp.69–93, and the bibliography it contains.

27. Pui Lan Kwok, 'God Weeps with our Pain' in John Pobee and Bärbel von Wartenbert-Potter (eds), *New Eyes for Reading: Biblical and Theological*

*Reflections by Women from the Third World*, Geneva: WCC 1986, pp.90–95.

28. In *Waiting on God*, London: Collins 1950, pp.122–23, Simone Weil wrote movingly of experiencing such affliction in her year in the factory, but did not develop the idea in connection with images of God.

29. *'kin-dom'* implies that we are all brothers and sisters in the new creation; see Ada Maria Isasi-Diaz, *En La Lucha/In the Struggle: Elaborating a Mujerista Theology*, Minneapolis: Fortress Press 1993, p.xi.

30. Christians of the second century saw in the martyred woman Blandina 'the One who was crucified for them'; cf. H. Musurillo (ed), *The Acts of the Christian Martyrs*, Oxford: Clarendon Press 1972, p.75. The North African slave, Felicitas, about to be thrown to the wild beasts of the arena after just giving birth to her baby, witnessed to Christ redemptively suffering within her; cf. P.Wilson-Kastner et al. (eds), *A Lost Tradition: Women Writers of the Early Church*, Washington DC: University Press of America 1981, pp.1–32.

31. I think especially of Lucy de Souza's painting of 'The Feminine Face of God' that depicts Christ/Christa as Tree of Life, surrounded by the four elements. This picture interweaves aspects of both Hindu and Christian spirituality in a very creative manner.

32. For a fuller account, see Susan Cole, Marian Ronan and Hal Taussig (eds), *Wisdom's Feast: Sophia in Study and Celebration*, Kansas City: Sheed and Ward 1996.

33. See Elizabeth Johnson, *She Who Is: The Mystery of God in Feminist Theological Discourse*, New York: Crossroad 1992, p.235.

34. See Elisabeth Schüssler Fiorenza, *Jesus: Miriam's Child, Sophia's Prophet*, New York: Continuum and London: SCM Press 1995, p.138 and Asphodel Long, *In a Chariot Drawn by Lions: The Search for the Female in Deity*, London: The Women's Press 1992, p.139.

35. See Ninna Beckman, 'Sophia, Symbol of Christian and Feminist Wisdom?', *Feminist Theology* 16, pp.32–54.

36. See Mary Grey, *The Wisdom of Fools? Seeking Revelation Today*, London: SPCK 1993.

37. See Celia Deane-Drummond, 'Sophia: The Feminine Face of God as a Metaphor for an Ecotheology', *Feminist Theology* 16, pp.11–31.

38. Elizabeth Johnson, *She Who Is*, pp.191–223.

# The Divine Exodus of God: Involuntarily Marginalized, Taking an Option for the Margins, or Truly Marginal?

MARCELLA ALTHAUS-REID

## Introduction: revolutions make theologians nervous

Josep Pla, the anti-clerical Catalan writer, recalls the following dialogue he had with one of his best friends, J. B. Solervicens, on religion and social change during the times of the Spanish civil war:

- *'Soler, we are conservative people . . .'*
- *'Correct. Revolutions make me nervous. We are conservative and moreover, we are poor . . .'*
- *'Would you be able to resolve such a contradiction? I don't believe it would be possible, not even using Hegelian dialectics . . .'*
- *'Excuse me! You have forgotten an important point. The situation is like this: we are conservative people, but we are poor and we are so hungry that it is scary (i tenim una gana que sparvera) . . . Terrible situation! Do you believe that it is possible to harmonize so many contradictions?'*
- *'This is a hell of a difficult task! Sometimes it looks as if Providence is tempting us . . .'*
  *And he said that with a sad and depressed countenance.*[1]

The task of finding theological explanations for people's hunger in order to keep everybody happy tends to fall invariably into the kind of contradiction which we are all, sadly, accustomed to. The so-called theologies of resignation, based on poverty and wealth distributed according to divine design, are part of the fabric of Christianity. However, these ways of thinking theology need to be linked not only to the presence of partisan economic interests in Christian institutions but to something more fundamental, such as a theological epistemology as the basis of these discussions. This theological epistemology presents us with a way of thinking permanently split between issues of loyalty to God and critical reality. God's goodness and power need to prevail over the presence of evil, such as the economic structures which disempower us. The resolution to this conflict is, as in the words of Pla, 'a hell of a task'. We are already familiar with this hell due to the critique of the place of ideology in theology. In Christianity, the justification of systems of oppression has come from interests related to the dynamics of wealth and power in society. At the same time, ideological discourses – and methods – have always found their way into theology, as a way of securing the convergence of hegemony and agency, including divine agency. 'The will of God' has been the ultimate historical glass ceiling of political discourses discouraging opposition. However, from the theologies of the consolation of the masses or resignation theologies, the subversiveness of the gospel eventually found the way to break the status quo of theology and ideology. Eventually, the message of the church as the opium of the masses showed interesting, contradictory effects too.

## I. The case of the involuntarily marginalized God

Let us consider, for instance, the fact that the encounter of 'God at the margins' in liberation theology came as the result of a surplus of the marginalization of God through ideological manipulations in theology. When we found the face of God amongst the poor, we did so because God had been marginalized from political discourses and theological discourses by default, which avoided the issue of the presence of God in the midst of people's economical sufferings. We may see that the ideological discourse of 'The Will of God' was the theodicy of a complacent, centrally located God comforting the hungry masses. It was the God who left, albeit temporarily, its centred location to go to the margins to explain how and why margins existed and fitted into creation theology. The margins were a necessity in the order of life created by God. As people needed to make sense of evilness, and for instance, of economic structures of evil from their own Christian perspective in order to survive, the theology of consolation was accepted. 'God' represented by hegemonic theologies went to the margins to explain things. Eventually, the unforeseen result from this was that from a theology of consolation grew a kind of faithful obstinacy or Christian stubbornness in people who had little reason to be Christian in the first instance. The arguments of consolation in theology changed according to different historical periods, but many people at the margins of church and society obstinately remained Christians.

That is the point with popular theology which is basically a theology of survival, and requires in its reflection the obstinate Christian faith which may convert to the desire to overcome injustices (social and economical for instance) by finding a spiritual and material superstructure which may somehow transform them. Popular theology comes from people who need the emotional strength not only to make sense of the presence of God in the world history of oppression, but to live the extra twenty-four hours of their lives which start without much hope of finding food, shelter or protection against violence. To find a reason literally to wake up every morning and to live an extra day is difficult when surrounded by any form of poverty and social exclusion due to racial, economic, cultural and sexually different constructions of reality. What is interesting here is that in circumstances of extreme marginalization (including the marginalization of the God of Liberation from 'politically indifferent' theologies), Christian people have found a space not of domestication but of struggle. That is, a space to locate the subversiveness of God in the margins. Even the simple allegorical read-ing of the Bible done to find God as a co-suffering friend, while at the same time finding consolation in the promise of change in their sufferings in the other world, is more subversive than it looks. This happens because the two basic assumptions of the readings are that God is an ally, and that faith has agency to change circumstances.

## II. God's option for the margins

These margins we are referring to then become the space of a complex negotiation of identities (human and divine) in theology. However, barter-ing pain for the promises of God as an ally and faith as instrumental to change has not always produced a shift in the understanding of a God who intervenes in history by generating disconformity and rebelliousness towards structures of oppression. Such was the task of liberation theologies, aiming to have a theology to accompany the poor and the marginalized, allowing their bartering process of making theological sense of injustice to continue while introducing critical realism in their reflections. This is the path from the marginalization of God by traditional theologies which created the margins in the first place, to the God at the margins, which chal-lenge why those margins existed. Paraphrasing Ché Guevara to synthesize the spirit of liberation theology in this point, we may say that the path from the marginalization of God to the God at the margins lies in the fact that we may become tougher, without losing our tenderness. Liberation theology was a tough theology which wanted to keep its tenderness, and in that tension, it was able to find God at the margins. The tough part was the questioning and the suspicion, which worked by not giving God an authority at the centre, as if Jesus at the margins was a vicar of a real Christ located somewere else.

On the contrary, the subversiveness of this praxis came from eventually pushing God to the margins out of their central identity. What happened was that the recognition of God at the margins was more an act of mapping God amongst the destitute than a re-discovery of an original God at the margins, and any important element which came from a theology at the margins therefore had these limitations. These were the limitations of the theological discourse at the centre challenged by marginalized experiences of life, but somehow struggling to retain their full central identity. For people with a good memory about the path of liberation theology in Latin America, it is enough to remember the struggle amongst Roman Catholic theologians concerned with the role of traditions when different interpretations of the Bible and the nature of the church came from popular Bible studies.[2] These difficulties illustrate the point of how different cultural and economic mediations still wanted to be part of any reflection from the so called 'margins' where theology was concerned. We are talking here of an unprecedent theological exodus in three stages: from a marginalized God, a God who was a mere good excuse for the justification of economic and cultural systems of exploitation, to a God at the margins. That God at the margins differs from the first in the fact that it is a God assuming the margins. That is God reclaiming a place, more than a displacement. That was the task of liberation theologies in general.

## III. Visions of a truly marginal God

However, the serious engagement of theology with people's struggles required another movement, this time from a God at the margins (still partaking of central definitions) to a more radical 'marginal God'. To move from the God at the margins to a marginal God (as one who does not deal with central discourses or identity processes) may be the task of a postcolonial theology, if that implies also the task of cutting ourselves free from Enlightenment conceptions of linear progress. Unfortunately postcolonial theology would produce the radical shift expected if its discourse is to be grounded in a disbalance so typical of post-Marxism which privileges culture over production. And in doing so, the marginality of people's experiences becomes reduced while the mechanisms of theological production remain untouched in terms of alienation and exploitation. The postcolonial subject is invoked but the marginal people do not gather and talk using their own voices and experiences as they did in liberation theologies. The question is, can neocolonial theologies ever depart from the master's references? We need to concede that God at the margins is a theologically geographical concept, and as such part of a master's map. It refers to a 'God out there' and rightly so; this is the God at the garbage dumps of South America and the God who accompanies people during the droughts in Africa. The God at the margins is the God who accompanies people in their suffering, but there is here an implicit original point of departure, an exodus of God from the point which, precisely, creates and defines the dualism of centre and marginality. By its mere presence, that God of the margins may be at risk of creating a new centre in the margins, with different themes and concerns but from an inherited point of view. The point is that this is the God of the people suffering from thirst, but not a thirsty God. The God who pities the children of the streets but not the God of the streets. A God at the margins, but not a marginal God.

What we should try to consider is whether, at the margins of church and theology, there are unauthorized sites of divinity. They project their shadow in theology in general and in liberation theologies in particular, as a deconstructive supplement of salvation. That is to say that those sites work as the subversive potential of theological discourses, in which fears of unfaithfulness in theological reflections and hopes for transformation keep bad company with each other. The God at the margins is a tame vision of the marginal God. It decentres power, but does not challenge it because the centre nurtures its epistemology. The God at the margins depends on the God at the centre, because one definition conditions the other. This is the reason why radical theologies at the margins can be politically enlightened yet oppresively sexist and racist at the same time. The centre way of knowing taints the margins with its authority, which this time is sacred authority.

However, the margins are not somehow 'out there' all the time. There are margins inside all of us, manifested in the difficult borders of, for instance, constructed sexuality and identity. There are untouched, seldom-addressed painful margins in the life of every Christian, which only a marginal God can address. The image of Jesus as a coal miner sharing his meagre lunch with fellow workers. The black Jesus or the Christa comes from this deep need of finding, not a God who sympathizes with our margins, but who belongs to them. However, the difficulties come from the epistemological presupposi-tions of our theological discourse.

The power of God in the margins is a power still relying on dependency. Without an assumed dependency relationship, and a dependency theology, there is no understanding of God. Even Jesus has been made to become an icon of dependency on God the Father. Dependency, the oneness of God and the unity and clarity of truth are the sacred trinity of theodicy, that is, the vindication of God as a creator of goodness from the history of people's oppression. The God at the margins seems sometimes to partake of the same project: to justify the divine existence which a degrading reality seems to deny, as if it were part of an old fashioned developmental model.

It is the marginal God's project which can lead us outside the develop-mental model in theology. If we have learned to become distrustful of developmental theories, conceived to organize the centre/peripheries model into a Christian project of solidarity, we should not use the same parameters in liberation theologies. In the world of development as liberation, we have privileged concepts such as mutually sustainable communities, interdepen-dency and self-reliance. Where do we find these concepts applied to the God of the excluded, of the theological reflections 'from the margins'? Margins are not margins but geographies in their own right. Margins as 'outside spaces' are illusory locations. What we call the discourses of the centre are just the edited texts of the rich and powerful, hegemonically organizing people's lifestyles with promises of salvation which exclude, for instance, economic salvation. Popular theology is therefore condemned to write only the addenda, remarks, notes at the margins of the page while the unjustified text of a different God is ignored.

## Conclusion: independence day

Sometime theology should declare an independence day, and start anew, from the real grassroots of marginal communities to find a God who is less domesticated, and less brainwashed than the displaced centre God now located at the margins of theological reflections. It should come from the struggles of the communities at the margins: poor communities, whose cultural and economical life has been obliterated or put under siege; com-munities marginalized on sexual and/or gender grounds, and all the marginalizations that hegemonic élites inflict on people. The concept of mutual dependency in relation to God may then supersede the monarchic conceptualization of the God-King, as by experience of community work, we may know that solidarity amongst equals is more important in communities of resistance than hierarchical dreams. As dialogue is one of the most precious elements of conscientization amongst marginalized people, the marginal God cannot be excluded from it. This is not a God who has the last word. That would be a grand narrative, not a God whose example in Jesus is of a constant conversation with people, asking their opinion and experiences and working from there. This is a God re-discovered in actions of social transformation and in conscientization processes. The marginal God may even encourage people's disloyalty towards the ideals of 'uniqueness' in favour of an understanding of plurality. Uniqueness has become the virtue of totalitarianism, not of democratic societies. Confronted with globalization processes, it will take a marginal God to show us that the best of our history of solidarity and strategical organization for change comes not from God's passion for the margins, as if this was God's vocation to visit the frontiers, but from a real location outside central constructions. The future of liberation and popular theologies may depend on this final understanding of the participation of the God at the margins with the projects of the centre. A truly 'marginal God' may have little common ground with the vicarious 'God of the poor' who, although visiting the margins, still lives far away and belongs to a central discourse of theology.

## Notes

1. Josep Pla, *Obras Completas*, Barcelona: Edicions Destino 1966, vol. 17, pp.557–58.
2. For a discussion on this point, cf. Marcella Althaus-Reid, 'Gustavo Gutiérrez went to Disneyland' in Fernando Segovia (ed), *Interpreting Beyond the Borders*, Sheffield: Sheffield University Press 2000, pp.36–57.

## Bibliography

David Batstone, Eduardo Mendieta et al. (eds), *Liberation Theologies, Postmodernity and the Americas*, London: Routledge 1997.

George De Schrijver (ed), *Liberation Theologies on Shifting Grounds*, Leuven: University of Leuven 1998.

# Songs of Desire:
# On Pop-Music and the Question of God

OLA SIGURDSON

Pop-culture is a vast field of cultural expression through many media, such as magazines, movies, music, television, etc. As it is not possible to cover every area of pop-culture, I will concentrate here on pop-music.

Let me first briefly clarify my understanding of pop-music. There are endless distinctions of genres in pop-music, and anyone who thinks that scholastic theology excesses in distinctions should make a comparison with these genres, of which I am no expert. If I instead stay with the broad genres, I suggest that it would not be wrong to label rock as well as country, blues, soul, hip-hop, etc. as pop-music. That is because all of them try to be popular in both the sense that they wish to communicate rather directly – i.e. without the requirement of much previous musical education on behalf of the listener – and in the sense that most pop-artists strive to be well known among public listeners. I certainly accept the challenge that there are huge differences between all these genres that I would like to call pop-music. I also concede that not all pop-music is direct in that it requires no explicitly educated taste, nor that the main purpose of all pop-musicians is to sell as many records as possible. However, I still think this minimal definition serves my purposes here, and I would merely wish to suggest that the popularity of pop-music has to do with the media revolution that started with the wireless radio in the first half of the twentieth century.

My thesis is that many, if not most, pop-music songs concern human desire, and that this is the point of contact with the question of God. The theme of desire for God as well as other human beings has, of course, always been one of the main themes of Christian theology. To name just one important theologian who reflected thoroughly on this theme: Augustine wrote a well-known investigation of desire in his *Confessions*.[1] Augustine would have recognized – even if not approved – much of what is being sung in pop-lyrics in our time.

## I. The hungry heart

Augustine wrote at the end of the fourth century that we should 'love, and do what we will',[2] and The Beatles sang in the 1960s, 'All you need is love'. In his *Confessions*, Augustine wrote: 'our hearts are restless till they find rest in Thee', while Bruce Springsteen still sings that 'everybody's got a hungry heart'. Generally speaking, one could say that love in pop-music is the happy or unfulfilled love of a human partner, whereas the Bible and Christianity focus on the love of God.

But even in pop-music, the associations are not entirely univocal. Can a human partner really satisfy the hunger of the heart that Springsteen sings about? On the one hand, we hear that 'Everybody needs a place to rest/ Everybody wants to have a home/ Don't make no difference what nobody says/ Ain't nobody like to be alone.'[3] But on the other hand, this need for companionship did not keep the singer at home: 'Got a wife and kids in Baltimore Jack/ I went out for a ride and I never went back/ Like a river that don't know where it's flowing/ I took a wrong turn and I just kept going.' The song 'Hungry Heart' offers no resolution, we hear of no sea that the river can flow into. Instead it expresses a longing, a kind of restlessness, on behalf of the person that the singer is impersonating. This is just one example of how pop-lyrics can assert the necessity, though insufficiency, of human love. And precisely this insufficiency has been reflected upon in theology.

According to much Christian theology, at least up until the early modern age, the reason for the sinful human condition lies in the fact that human beings try to satisfy their hunger with what cannot satisfy it in any real sense. Money, sex, power are just simulacra that simulate – each on its own or all together – the road to enjoyment of the highest good. Yet since these are finite goods, they cannot satisfy the infinite or spiritual hunger that constitutes human beings. Instead they lure us humans to search for true happiness in an ever-increasing consumption of money, sex and power. The stakes are raised all the time, but they never truly satisfy this hunger, nor do they channel this hunger to its true source. Money, sex and power easily become idols, i.e. something that promises more than it can hold, and lead human beings astray. The only true answer to the spiritual hunger of human beings is provided by God, since only God, who is eternal, can match a hunger that is infinite. Everything else, everything finite falls short of this infinite hunger, since it puts limits on it. Therefore, it is not entirely correct to speak of the 'satisfaction' of the hungry heart, since this sounds as if the desire would cease. It is more appropriate, theologically speaking, to talk about the intensification of *true* desire, an intensification that corresponds to its transcendent object. This love of God as the true desire of human beings breaks the slavery of the idols. This does not mean that money, sex or power should be regarded as intrinsically evil. The problem is that they are finite things, and therefore they do not measure up to an infinite hunger.

It is hard to avoid the reflection that in our time it seems to be the poets and the songwriters rather than the theologians that know how to articulate this human hunger. Not that the poets or the songwriters are saying exactly the same thing as what, for instance, Augustine said. But they, like him, know what is important in our lives: love, hope, trust, failure, death. In modern society the drama of life has been privatized, whereas consumption and production have defined the essence of human beings. In late-modern society reason and desire have been understood as opposites. But the poets and the songwriters have publicly thematized the prominent place of desire in our lives. Through their lyrics they have also shown, in ways similar to the story of Cain and Abel in Genesis or the story of David, Uriah and Bat-Seeba in II Samuel, which destructive consequences human desire can have.

Sometimes pop-music tries to tell us something about God. More often it does not. But associations to the Bible, to Christianity or to some other religion are quite frequent. This is not very surprising if one considers the common theme of human desire, and also the deep impression which two millennia of Christian history has made in the West. It is true what the journalist Jack Miles wrote in his book *God: A Biography* concerning the anonymous presence of God in modern Western society: 'His is the restless breathing we still hear in our sleep.'[4] This goes for pop-music as well, certainly not only for some kind of 'Christian' pop-music, but also for pop-music in general. There are a lot of common topics, far beyond any particular Christian genre of pop-music. Let me mention some examples and at the same time comment on the popularity of pop-music.

## II. The meaning of pop-music

What makes a good song? My hypothesis is that the lyrics in pop- and rock-music, more than in novels or stories, have a lot to do with emotive expressions rather than cognitive reflection or information. To generalize, a 'classic' pop-song is about three minutes long, and therefore has a short time to attract attention. It does so through evoking an emotive response, which is heightened through the repetition of the refrain. A good pop-song is often quite intensive, in a sense that few other artistic genres could measure up to. This – of course very general judgment – does not mean that pop-music is without content or is trivial, i.e. that its message just is 'itsy bitsy teenie weenie yellow polka dot bikini'. But it does mean that the emotive intensity belongs to the nature of pop-music.

It has not been concealed to the writers of pop-lyrics that allusions to the Bible or to religious motives could heighten the intensity of a pop-song. The lyric-writers who are skilled in their craft do not necessarily quote the Bible text as it stands, rather they use its imagery to weave their own stories. Let me take an example that might be unknown to readers of this article, but which is nevertheless suitable, because I could use it to illustrate what I am hinting at from my own experience. The Swedish songwriter Plura Jonsson, singer and songwriter in the band Eldkvarn, has in the record *Utanför lagen* (Out of law) from 1985 in the song 'Landsortsgrabb' (Country-boy) written the following line (my translation): 'the book of life has its better pages'.[5] This is probably an allusion to that book of life that is mentioned twice in Revelation (3.5; 20.15). According to Revelation, one would not want to be erased from that book.

I think this is a brilliant line of poetry which Plura has given us. On the one hand, he shows a sense of his own shortcomings compared to the better pages of the book. On the other hand, he also expresses some kind of hope, since the singer at least has not been erased from the book of life – his name remains there, however weak the ink that has written it may be.

One could, of course, question my interpretation and claim that I make associations of which the writer of the song was not aware, and therefore over-interpret the song. Perhaps the book of life is a metaphor conceived by Plura himself. Is it then proper for a theologian to claim that Plura maybe is not as original as he thought he would be, through putting his text in a context that he – perhaps – was not aware of or did not want to associate with? I certainly would not want to claim that Plura was not a good song-writer or unable to invent his own metaphors. What I would like to claim is that it is not very important if 'the book of life' in this song is Plura's own metaphor or not. In one obvious sense it is, since he is the writer of this song. But still, our entire language is built on metaphors and associations. Those who write song-lyrics are probably not unaware that they use more or less conscious associations to build up a lyric. I presume that the writing of pop-lyrics on the whole is a rather intuitive process. It would hardly do to deduce or in some other way reason one's way towards the apt metaphor. To be a good writer of lyrics, one must have the 'feel' for it. This means that many associations are unconscious to the songwriter, or perhaps become conscious afterwards, through the interpretations of them by others. Literary theorists speak of 'intertextuality', and we could also say, more poetically, that all literary texts in our culture speak to each other and thus nourish each other through the expansion of their respective horizons of interpretation.

It could well be that I as a theologian associate Plura's metaphor 'the book of life' to the Bible because I am a theologian, and in a certain sense deal with 'the book of life' in my daily work. My thoughts follow theological traces, and I hear what I want to hear, or what I am taught to hear. But still I would like to defend my right to associate to the Bible, notwithstanding whether or not Plura did so in our example. The message of something with the intensity of a good pop-song is highly dependent upon the context of listening. Think of someone speaking of a song as 'our song': 'Darling, do you remember, this was the song they played the first time we met?' Another example: 'This song reminds me of high-school.' Yet another: 'This is perfect music for listening to while driving a car.' The associations we make are dependent on the context in which we are listening. A rather banal song that does not mean anything for one person might speak of love and happiness or perhaps failure or death to another. I think one could argue that a pop-song is quite open to interpretation, and thus could be made sense of in a lot of different contexts and a lot of different moods. As far as I am concerned Plura's songs have been important for my own existential reflections on what it means to be a Christian, and quite independent of whatever intention Plura might have had. 'The book of life has its better pages' – thus have I thought often.

I should think that the popularity of pop-music has to do both with its intensity and its openness to different interpretations. It is simply useful for a lot of people in a lot of different situations. Indeed, much of pop-music is commercialized, but this does not stop the listener from taking it out of its commercial context and relating it to existentially more significant situations. It is, of course, a delicate question how colonized our structures of desire are by commercial forces. I still think, however, that we have the ability of 'making do' with commercial products in spite of their commerciality, and thus make them our own in an existentially significant way.[6]

Madonna, who certainly has earned the title of a commercially aware popmusician, in her lyrics in the album *Ray of Light* of 1998 uses associations to several religions, especially Hinduism.[7] It is entirely possible that she makes use of them for commercial reasons – religion sells. But still the songs tell about giving up one's self-centredness and of learning how to say no to what momentarily satisfies one's desires in order to win something greater through true love. In the song 'Nothing really matters' we hear allusions to Augustine as well as to The Beatles: 'Nothing really matters/ Love is all we need/ Everything I give you/ all comes back to me.' And when Madonna in her mega-hit 'The Power of Goodbye' sings: 'Freedom comes when you learn to let go/ Creation comes when you learn to say no', it is obvious that her song is about the power that lies in the ability to say no. According to this song, devouring everything that comes one's way does not constitute love. Love can take farewell, and thus avoid being transformed into a perversion of love. Perhaps Augustine would have been put off by the image that Madonna has built around her own person, but he would surely have understood what she sings about.

### III. That God-shaped hole

If my thesis is correct that pop-music and Christian faith have a common theme in human desire, and if the Bible and other Christian texts are not unknown to the writers of pop-lyrics, then what does this mean for the theological question of God? To start with, it does at least mean that there is something to talk about. There are several common themes that interest both church and pop-*aficionados*. These themes do not only concern us in our everyday life in more or less secular societies, not only in our sexuality and relationships with other human beings, not only in our hunger for justice, but also, in and with all these other themes, in the love of God. Of course, this is a highly generalized view of pop-music. Each author of lyrics and each composer of music has his or her own personal relation – or lack of relation – to the question of God and to Christianity and its images of God. But even if I might not be able to show it conclusively here, I believe that these are common themes, and so obvious in many pop-songs that they do not deserve to be neglected.

To begin with, it is usually not pop-music's task to offer a very 'orthodox' picture of God in music and lyrics. More often than not songwriters feel free to borrow imagery from different religions. Madonna's *Ray of Light* is a prime example of 'syncretism' in music, but still is just an example of a common trend. However, there are counter-examples. During the last few years many well-known artists have recorded music that offers a quite straightforward picture of their own personal religious (not necessarily Christian) confessions. The images of God presented by pop-music are quite varied to say the least.

Be that as it may, I do believe one could generalize with regard to one common theme that concerns the question of God in contemporary pop-music, namely the search for what it means to be an authentic human being. For most pop-music God is seldom or never an abstract theme, like in some theology, sermons or hymns. We seldom find a reflection upon God's attributes outside of some intense personal or social context. God is most often called upon in relation to the quest for authentic selfhood. The famous Irish group U2 provides us with an example. Several of the members in this group have publicly declared themselves to be Christians. This fact has been quite obvious in their lyrics, too, even if this theme has been darker in the 1990s, and sometimes even outright cynical.

In 1997 U2 released the album *Pop*, which then was followed by a world tour. The album *Pop* is full of spiritual quests and questions, tightly inter-woven with a haunting and rather complex music.[8] In the album's third song, 'Mofo', we hear the singer Bono express his spiritual longing: 'lookin' for to save my soul / lookin' in the places where no flowers grow/ lookin' for to fill that God-shaped hole'. With the help from a quotation from Jean-Paul Sartre this songs expresses a longing for an authenticity or even purity that seems to be gone forever: 'still looking for the face I had before the world was made'.

If 'Mofo' expresses the spiritual longing for authenticity, we have in the fourth song 'If God will send his angels' the question whether God really could answer this quest for authenticity. The singer declares that no one else is to blame but yourself – 'nobody made you do it, no one put words in your mouth' – and asks whether everything would be all right if God sent his angels. The answer to the question is ambivalent: 'God has his phone off the hook, babe, would he even pick it up if he could?' Even the Christian message has been contaminated by the way it has been handled: 'Jesus never let me down you know Jesus used to show me the score/ then they put Jesus in show business now it's hard to get in the door.' This song expresses some doubts as to whether God really will or can help in the search for authenti-city. But the problem might as well be what has been done in God's name when 'they put Jesus in show business'.

In the album's last song, 'Wake up dead man', we again hear a call to Jesus for help. 'Jesus, Jesus help me/ I'm alone in this world/ and a fucked up world it is too.' But we still here some doubts about God: 'Jesus, I'm waiting here boss/ I know you're looking out for us/ but maybe your hands aren't free/ your Father, He made the world in seven/ He's in charge of heaven/ will you put a word in for me.' The refrain explicitly calls on Jesus to do something: 'Wake up dead man.' The call for Jesus' help seems not to be entirely confident of his help. Even if one makes a link to the resurrection in this call for the dead man to wake up, one could also hear some dissatisfaction with someone that is supposed to help, but is not awake to the afflictions and confusions of humanity. Where is Jesus when all is dark? Is he still dead?

As a whole, *Pop* is a minor masterpiece when it comes to expressing the spiritual longing of humanity in relationship to contemporary questions about authentic selfhood. These questions – in U2's lyrics – are connected to failures in personal human relationships, but also to the chaos of a world that seems to move faster all the time and where famine and political disasters are everyday news. One could, of course, quote a number of artists or records where the answer of God is more obvious, or where the tone is even darker, but what is interesting with this album is the often very profound combination of faith *and* doubt, of sensuality *and* spirituality. 'So where is the hope and where is the faith . . . and the love?' is the question that U2 puts to its listeners in 'If God will send his angels'. The question receives no final answer in *Pop*.

To conclude, with regard to the question of God in pop-music I suggest that the common denominator is the quest for what it means to be an authentic human being. This quest often – not always – calls upon God or some higher spiritual being for help. As in U2's *Pop*, there could be doubts about the likelihood of God's help and thus about the possibility of ever accomplishing human wholeness. But this does not mean that 'that God-shaped hole' is denied. The expressions of it are (almost) as varied as there are writers of pop-music. It could be articulated in more or less vague ways and the transcendent dimension could be emphasized more or less. But the pervasiveness of this theme – hinted at rather than shown in this article – suggests that this might be a very important insight for the contemporary theological dialogue between church and pop-music.

## Notes

1. Cf. ch.1 'Augustinus Hunger' (Augustine's Hunger) in my book *Hungerns väg: Om Gud, kyrka och mångfald* (The Way of Hunger: On God, Church and Plurality), Lund: Arcus 2000, and the references in this chapter.
2. Augustine, *In epistolam Ioannis*, VIII.7.
3. 'Hungry Heart' was originally released on Bruce Springsteen's album *The River*, Columbia 1980.
4. Jack Miles, *God: A Biography*, New York: Alfred A. Knopf 1995, p.408.
5. Eldkvarn, *Utanför lagen*, EMI 1986.

6. Cf. Michel de Certeau, *The Practice of Everyday Life*, Berkeley/Los Angeles/London: University of California Press 1984, pp.15–42.
7. Madonna, *Ray of Light*, Maverick 1998.
8. U2, *Pop*, Island 1997.

# II.  Changing Perceptions of God in Interpreting the Bible and Christian Tradition

# 'God is Relationship': Some Recent Approaches to the Mystery of the Trinity

The attempt to think of God in terms of relationship, which is traditional in Christian theology,[1] is becoming topical again in post-modernity. In fact it is coupled with a diagnosis of the present moment, which many people feel to be a 'turning point'. The modern era is said to have been stamped with the emancipation of the 'bourgeois' subject from his or her natural and traditional constraints, in particular religious constraints, a development which has been made possible by a critical way of thinking. Today we are supposed to be more aware of the disastrous consequences of this secular approach to reality: two world wars, the holocaust, and the immense ecological damage that has been done are thought to have led us to examine our consciences. The relations between men and women; the structures of participation in our societies; the relationships between continents, cultures and religions; and respect for nature need to be promoted by a way of thinking in terms of difference which is more modest about the absolute claims made by European culture and more concerned that those with different perspectives should be good neighbours.

It is in the framework of such a diagnosis that Latin theology, above all since Peter Lombard (1095–1160), is often accused of having made the mystery of the Trinity and monotheism more and more bloodless. Consequently, it is argued, Latin theology is partly responsible for the West's obsession with unity, which makes it have less respect for the multiple differences and breaks that mark its culture and its internal and external relations. Even the founders of contemporary trinitarian theology, Karl Barth and Karl Rahner, would not escape this charge. Did not Barth try to understand the doctrine of the Trinity as a simple explicitation of the event of revelation which is summed up in the unitary formula 'God reveals himself as the Lord'?[2] And did not Rahner improperly give priority to the mystery of Unity, seeing the Trinity implied in his definition of Christianity as the 'religion of immediate relationship to God'?[3] The accusation of 'idealist modalism' pronounced over these two great masters is evidently based on their reservations about the concept of 'person', which has been so transformed by the modern 'subject' that it could be applied to God only in his unity, on pain of lapsing immediately into tritheism.

Here readers will have recognized the diagnosis of Jürgen Moltmann, who in 1980 was one of the first to have indicated a turning point within trinitarian theology, in his book *The Trinity and the Kingdom of God*.[4] His critique of the God who does not suffer had been known since 1972; now, in the first volume of his systematic theology, devoted to the triune God, he took one step further by moving rigorously from a 'psychological' to a 'social' doctrine of the Trinity. He did this with a critique of all hierarchical systems, whether political or ecclesiastical, which are almost always founded on a patriarchal monotheism. Others, like Leonardo Boff, have followed him,[5] and some have even preceded him. In the Catholic tradition, the revaluation of the biblical and patristic concept of *koinonia* or *communio* by the Second Vatican Council in fact provoked a good deal of reflection on the communion within the Trinity. The 'theses for a trinitarian ontology' put forward by Klaus Hemmerle, Bishop of Aachen, developed in 1976 in connection with his reading of the work of Hans Urs von Balthasar,[6] are a characteristic expression of this. They are all the more interesting, as the attempt to reconstruct an ontology puts the Trinity in principal position not only with relation to all theology (as Barth and Rahner already wanted) but also in connection with a whole vision of the world. Thus here trinitarian thought meets up with the controversial question of the diagnosis of the present moment.

It is precisely this point that I want to discuss in this article, by referring to one of the great syntheses of recent years, Gilbert Greshake's 'trinitarian theology'.[7] In a way it is a symbol of the turning point I have just mentioned. I shall begin by sketching out the main lines of this theology; then I shall bring out three points in the discussion to spell out where the difficulty of thinking of God as relationship lies today; finally, I shall suggest another way of approaching the mystery of God from our life together in societies shaken by globalization, where cultural and social differences have been increasingly exacerbated.

## I. 'The triune God'

Gilbert Greshake's trinitarian theology in fact represents more than just a new development of the dogmatic treatise *De Deo uno et trino*. The author wants to bring trinitarian faith out of its isolation and to relate it to human experience: on the one hand he considers how it could open up the potentialities of creation, illuminate the obscurity of human experience, clarify the aporias of the world, and so on; on the other hand he seeks to show how these manifestations of the trinitarian God reveal the inner life of God. The aim of this 'method of correlation' is to develop 'an integral vision of reality in a trinitarian perspective' (p.25) and to show its plausibility in relation to other visions of the world.

He also first expounds 'the way towards a trinitarian theology of communion'. Is not the crucial problem of trinitarian theology the relationship between unity and plurality in God, a problem which the West has largely underestimated in giving priority to a unitary way of thinking? To arrive at an interpersonal image of God which understands God as the Communion of life and love, it is therefore necessary to retrace the history of the concept of person and try to discover in it traces of a dialogical and communitarian conception which can help towards a balanced understanding of the unity and plurality in God. This brings us to the central thesis of the book:

> That God is triune signifies that God is this Communion in which the three divine persons realize, in a trialogical play of love, the one divine life as mutual self-communication. It is not necessary to appeal either to a substantial unity which would 'precede' (logically) this relational play of the three persons (the Latin model), or to a unity realized in the Father and communicated by him to the two other persons (the oriental model); it is rather the *Communio* as a process of mediation between unity and reality that is the *original and inseparable* reality of the one divine life (in philosophical language: of the unique *actus purus* of the being who proves in his essence to be 'communicative'). The divine life therefore implies the different moments of the realization of this unique event of mutual communication and thus at the same time both unity and plurality (p.179).

The author rightly emphasizes the analogical character of trinitarian discourse (pp.179–82). This also signifies that the concept of person, which is accessible to basic human experience, enters the horizon of understanding and reflection only after it has been given to humankind by revelation.

Since the Trinity must be considered the principle of all theology, in the second part of his work Greshake applies his 'trinitarian key' to different facets of the Christian mystery: the relationship between creator and creature, the historical realization of revelation – the author speaks of the drama of the Trinity – and the church as a mystery of trinitarian *koinonia*.

In this article I would want to emphasize above all the long section on creation (pp.219–325). The main decision consists in considering creation to be primarily situated at the very heart of the trinitarian communion: 'in fact, the purely natural order does not exist' (p.37). So only the idea of the Trinity allows us to understand the specific difference of creation, not in a negative way as a 'lack of being', but positively, from the difference *in* God himself. The author spells out this conception by making overflowing love the origin (not necessarily because it is already given within the Trinity): it is this love that authorizes the freedom and autonomy of the creature by withdrawing, giving it space and time. In terms of the Trinity, the paradox of the confrontation between God and his creation and God's simultaneous immanence in it is in fact based on the relationship between the Father and the Son and the in-habitation of the Spirit. It is the second decision of this chapter which pushes to extremes the initial idea of the work, namely that revelation offers the believer an 'integral horizon of experience' (p.29). While being polemical about a conception of secularization which is unilaterally based on the difference (p.238), the author therefore wants to make reality 'transparent' to the trinitarian communion. Thus he deciphers the *vestigia Trinitatis* both in the *structures* of reality (matter and human life, with a quite abstract conception of sexuality, for example without reference to fatherhood) and in its *becoming* (going as far as a trinitarian understanding of the theory of evolution and the history of the world), without anywhere discussing the permanent risk of a gnosis.

We should again note that the treatment of the entry of God into history, in this same chapter on creation, allows him to maintain the Scotist thesis about the motive for the incarnation and at the same time to go on to maintain the dramatic character of the economy of salvation. This he develops very broadly in the footsteps of Balthasar's 'theodramatics', which also investigates the conditions for sin in God. Thus the distinction between nature and supernature, rejected as abstract at the beginning of the book, recurs here, in a way, at another level: the 'trinitarization' of the real, the structures of which the author has just analysed in the chapter on creation, also 'abstracts' sin and its healing. These are treated only in the second part, which follows.

In the last part of his very long discussion, Greshake finally leaves the 'internal world' of the mysteries of Christianity – in the logic of the chapter on creation – to show that trinitarian faith can also function as a hermeneutical key which makes it possible to illuminate and resolve a number of problems that arise in (post-)modern societies. In the last resort these are all about the difficulty of dealing with the relation between unity and plurality. After developing the basis of an ontological Trinity, in succession he deals with the correlations between religion and society in the framework of a renewed political theology, and with the modern critique of religious and interfaith dialogue. Each time he shows how his trinitarian theology helps to deal with these well-known aporias of moderity.[8]

## II. Correlation and analogy

Greshake's work certainly stands out for its breadth, the wealth of its documentation and the ambition, indeed the force, of its main thesis. The brief survey which I have just given has passed over many points, in particular the discussions of christology, eschatology and ecclesiology; it has been interested more in the impressive global coherence and construction and the decisions taken by the author. He has chosen the approach by creation, the counterpart to 'the integral horizon of human experience', in order to insert his 'trinitarian key' into the cosmos of the Christian mysteries and his integral view of the world. This is the weak point at which trinitarian theology – like all theology – is marked and perhaps damaged by the present moment, the place where the 'method of correlation' comes in. The coherence of Greshake's presentation therefore helps us to discuss his decisions and to suggest some reflections on the methodological and theological conditions for a contemporary development of the Trinity.

### *1. Respecting the radical autonomy of the real and the plurality of cultures*

From an epistemological point of view[9] the author, who uses the support of other disciplines (the sciences, the human sciences and philosophy) in his global construction, makes use – without really discussing it – of a 'model of integration' (which is quite typical of certain post-modern tendencies). This takes too little notice of what Kant called the 'limits' between disciplines.[10] Granted, he refers to Eberhard Jüngel's expression 'experience *with* experience' (pp.30ff.), in order to point out the correlation between human experience of the real and trinitarian revelation, but he does so without the

Tübingen theologian's sensitivity to the different levels of human language, and notably the essential difference between metaphorical (or parabolic) language and scientific conceptuality. His 'integral vision of the world in a trinitarian perspective' is thus more like a homogeneous representation (even in his remarks on art). Under cover of an approach in terms of communion, it conveys the idea of a Catholic culture.

While respecting this choice, we may ask whether the trinitarian faith of Christians is necessarily constitutive of a *Catholic culture*. Can we not understand it, particularly in secular societies, as a way of placing oneself *in relationship to and in a plurality of cultures*? So it needs to be approached less as 'vision', 'representation', 'global society' or 'key' than as a *style* of communication, of the *attraction* of the gospel or again a *mode of being* in the church and in society; that would make it possible to pay more respect, not to independence but to the autonomy and the difference at the levels of the real and the specific languages which make it up.

## 2. *Starting from Jesus of Nazareth's experience of God*

This epistemological discussion, which I have only sketched out, then has repercussions for the treatment of the scriptures. The author's 'integral' approach is in fact marked by a lack of sensitivity in his work to the differentiated economy of the scriptures. It could be argued that the whole of the second part is devoted to the history of salvation, and that is true. But the *biblical form* of this economy, for example the amazing diversity of the christological and pneumatological approaches, is from the start *unified* by the conceptuality of communion.[11] Here we have the persistence of a unitary way of thinking! The decisive point is in fact the transition from the 'basic' experience of the New Testament, which the author describes in terms of Eastern theology that identifies God with the Father( p.49), to the trinitarian formula (pp.49–50). In reality this short-circuits the attempts of the New Testament to state the identity of the 'mediating figures' of Jesus and the Spirit with the terminology of the Word and of Wisdom.This transition, which anticipates the author's thesis, is all the more decisive, since it continually relativizes the negative reservations of official trinitarian theology in favour of a positive understanding (pp.56–61). In any case, we should note that other approaches, which start more from the *experience of God* granted to Jesus of Nazareth, Christ and Son, and to his disciples and apostles, are possible here.

*3. Unicity and relationship do not exclude each other but mutually reinforce each other*

Finally, at the strictly trinitarian level, the conceptual homogenization of the image of God[12] beyond what is said in the New Testament necessarily raises the problem of analogy. Greshake locates the analogy solely between the *communio* at the heart of creation and the trinitarian *communio* (pp.179–82). But greater attention to the theologies of the New Testament would have made him more sensitive to the analogy *within* the Trinity. Father, Son and Spirit are not 'person' in the same way, as Rahner and Schoonenberg[13] had already stated quite forcefully. If we are to remain sensitive to this analogy within the Trinity and critical of images of God in terms of family, friends or communion, are we not forced to follow Barth and Rahner in giving up the concept of 'person' when speaking of the 'three' and addressing them in prayer? Did not Rahner say in his famous article of the same name that in the New Testament *Theos* denotes the first person of the Trinity? But it has to be maintained that the unicity of the Father and the unicity of the Son are not to be numbered – they are incomparable – and that their relationship to each other is again of a quite different order.

The schematic enumeration of these three points in the discussion is meant to point out the difficulties of *thinking of God effectively as relationship*. The 'differentiation' which characterizes Western reality invites us first of all to take quite seriously the anti-Gnostic statement *par excellence* that God is mystery: God reveals nothing that we could know by ourselves. God reveals himself as an utterly discreet mystery – a 'voice', one might say, at the very beginning of the dawning of our own freedom of conscience in relation to other consciences, a voice which resounds as far as our limited experiences of violence, lies and death. It is on the basis of this theological pre-understanding that the Bible is to be read, in its very diversity, in a relational interplay between readers and others, an interplay which today 'reproduces' the attraction of the relationship between Jesus, Christ and Son, his followers, and many others who are grappling with the mysterious fatherhood of God. This relational interplay – which in the early church was called the 'economy' – is then experienced by believers as 'trinitarian' revelation. Here the analogy is the guardian of the mystery of relationship, in which the relationship and unicity of each of the 'persons' is not exclusive, but each reinforces the other. Only the Old and New Testament terminology about 'holiness' allows us to approach both the style of this relational interplay and the mystery of God which it reveals without damaging the radical autonomy of the created and the different orders of reality. I shall now go on to sketch this out, though I cannot do justice to all the anthropological elements which are called for in a reflection on the relationship.

## III. Relationship as holiness: the thrice holy God

### *1. What is holiness?*

The holiness of certain human figures of the past and present, in the first place that of Jesus of Nazareth, in fact always seem to evoke a good deal of admiration, even beyond the frontiers of institutional Christianity. That is easily understood if we recall the two inseparable facets of holiness which the scriptures allow us to discern in the history of humanity.

Here in fact we meet people capable of creating radiance simply by their presence alone, because in them thought, words and actions are in absolute agreement in a kind of simplicity of conscience which the Gospels describe by talking of someone whose 'yes is yes' and whose 'no is no'. If their 'authenticity' is the inner aspect of holiness, at the same time it results in a relational context which Luke and Matthew spell out on the basis of the famous Golden Rule: 'Whatever you wish that men would do to you, do so to them; for this is the law and the prophets' (Matt. 7.12). This rule is in no way peculiar to the New Testament: it exists in Judaism, in Greek and Chinese culture and so on; it is still put forward in the great debates on justice and human rights.[14] As a simple indicator of the basic reciprocity which governs our human relations, it presents itself first as a maxim of respect and justice, a summary of the law. But it discreetly appeals to an amazing attitude, the paradoxical capacity to 'put oneself in the place of another' without leaving one's own place, again in a particular concrete situation. This happens when someone shows active sympathy and compassion to others – 'Who is my neighbour?' . . . My neighbour is the one to whom I come close by an inordinate reversal which can never be asked for but which is offered in a particular unexpected situation (Luke 10.25–36). Here someone else's perspective is adopted to the point of taking that person's violence upon oneself (Matt. 5.23ff.). So holiness according to the Gospels is the unbounded fulfilment of the Golden Rule – the summary of the law and the prophets – which takes to the limit the consistency of the subject with itself: the simplicity of the heart. Here radiance is subordinated to a capacity to efface oneself for the benefit of others.

Do we understand the force of this action, which many people feel to be utterly necessary, at a time when globalization, an extreme awareness of social and cultural differences, and the violence which results from them, subject our life together to a harsh test? When we realize that the future of the globe depends not only on a global justice which is in itself difficult to conceive, but on human figures and communities capable of living according to the truth of their consciences and exposing themselves to the violence of others without retaliating with the same weapons, we all at once 'measure' the miraculous character of the effective and infinitely diversified emergence of these attitudes in our history. They are absolutely miraculous because they cannot be required in any way.

## 2. *Access to holiness or the emergence of the incomparable uniqueness of every being*

I have just shown how in the Judaeo-Christian tradition 'holiness' qualifies the understanding of *relationship*: I still have to explain how the 'emergence of the *incomparable uniqueness* of each being' – of the person, as the ancients put it – is the condition of access to a relational interplay which can be marked by holiness.

Given the finite condition of our existence, the uniqueness of living beings has a fundamental ambivalence: instead of being felt as a gift, the awareness of finitude and the call to accept one's own uniqueness are often the places where there is a tendency for people's 'fear of being' to appear: this provokes their jealousy, not to say their violence. We would like to compare our lives, and this presupposes an imaginary common 'measure'. Though this comparison should lead us towards the incomparable 'beyond measure' which is represented by the uniqueness of each individual, it constantly slides towards jealousy and ends up in violence which seizes the lives of others for the benefit of its own. What then proves miraculous is the birth of the 'courage to be' in a subject. It happens when people suddenly discover, always through a meeting with someone else, that the 'beyond measure' of their uniqueness' – which makes them afraid – is in reality 'in its measure' a real cure for their temptation to compare themselves with others and marks the emergence of a force of conscience which is capable of fulfilling the Golden Rule and of perceiving, in such circumstances, that effacing itself for the benefit of others allows it to become what it is. That which is beyond any comparison, and is attained at the moment of such an event – the victory over violence – simultaneously makes both relationship and uniqueness possible. It does so in a process which truly constitutes the 'person' by an adjustment, beyond any comparison and never achieved, of that which is beyond measure in every human existence to the measure that it gives itself.

## 3. God as holiness which communicates itself

The amazement at the 'miraculous' holiness of a multitude of human figures of the past and present allows us to understand the identity and work of Jesus of Nazareth from within. In fact his public way begins with episodes of healing, all of which show, in their amazing richness, how he communicates to those interested in the 'courage to be' that I have just mentioned, the possibility of a holiness of life that can never be foreseen. To those who cross his way Jesus transmits his own identity, what the Gospel texts call his *dynamis*: we could translate it now as his health and holiness, at any rate his vital energy, which our scriptures describe by the term 'spirit'. He gives it freely to a multitude of men and women, letting them go their own way, even sending the majority of them back without tying them to him or to one another in the bond of disciple and master. He engenders people who discover their own depths in freedom of conscience. This is suggested magnificently by the paradoxical remark addressed to a woman: '*My* daughter, it is *your* faith that has saved you' (Mark 5.34). This liberality announces the unheard-of wealth of the acts of holiness in our history, a holiness which can never be imprisoned within the limits of the Christian tradition. This openness in return makes Jesus' own holiness credible: for him the ultimate temptation would have been the diabolical suggestion that he should (want to) remain the only one of his kind – 'Unless a grain of wheat falls into the earth and dies, it remains alone; but if it dies, it bears much fruit' (John 12.24) – whereas he desires to share his identity integrally and equally with his followers and many others. It is only the miraculous access of each of them to his or her own uniqueness, to a 'courage to be' with unlimited dimensions that are revealed through the most hidden actions for the benefit of others, that makes it possible to enter into this desire of Jesus and to understand suddenly that this desire, which is at the same time absolutely unique and universal, makes him 'the holy one of God' (John 6.69).

The holy one *of God*? Not only in the sense that we would want to give an absolute origin to the 'miracle' of holiness in our history, but above all because we then ourselves hear, at the depth of our own consciences when they are coming to grips with the life of others, a discreet and convincing voice which murmurs in such circumstances – and these are sometimes dramatic – a 'happy are you'. This voice can only be that of God 'the Father' who finds his joy in sharing holiness, and that is its very essence.

The thrice-holy God (Rev. 4.8) thus reveals himself in the basic experience that I have just described: silence belongs to the Father, the holiness is that of his only Son and his followers in our history – the Word of the Father which is silent after having said *everything* and given *everything* in his Son – the 'consolation' which makes possible this holiness that communicates itself is the work of the Spirit of God. Does this historical experience, graciously open to the readers of the Bible, give them access to the very intimacy of God, to God as relationship? Rahner's axiom claims that 'the Trinity which manifests itself in the economy of salvation is the immanent Trinity, and vice versa'. In the perspective of this article, particularly in the discussion of the three points in the second part, we must simply state that this identification between the historical economy and the intimacy of God presupposes that the 'silence' of God, so characteristic of modern differentiation, is not discredited by a post-modern religious discourse but honoured as the highest mark of respect. Scripture is read as creating a style of multiform communication because it is rooted in the 'holiness' of Jesus of Nazareth, and the analogy, above all that within the Trinity, is understood as giving access to the kingdom of the incomparable.[15] So we can understand that there is no contradiction in maintaining that in God the 'original relationships' do not create any hierarchical order but a bond of parity between those who are unique (Rev. 22.1). This is an unexpected hope for a humanity many of whose children have to live with teeth on edge because they have eaten too many green grapes left by their parents.

*Translated by John Bowden*

## Notes

1. Cf. Thomas Aquinas, *STh* I a, q.29, a 4, and Richard of St Victor, *The Trinity*, Book III, 19 (for a historical survey cf. B. J. Hilberath, *Der Personbegriff der Trinitätstheologie in Rückfrage von Karl Rahner zu Tertullians 'Adversus Praxeam'*, Innsbruck and Vienna 1986).
2. Karl Barth, *Church Dogmatics I.1, The Doctrine of the Word of God*, Edinburgh 1932.
3. Karl Rahner, *Grundkurs des Glaubens*, Freiburg 1976; id., 'Der dreifaltige Gott als transzendenter Urgrund der Heilsgeschichte', *Mysterium Salutis* II, Einsiedeln 1967, pp.317–401.
4. Jürgen Moltmann, *The Trinity and the Kingdom of God*, London and New York 1981, pp.129–77.

5. Leonardo Boff, *Trinity and Society*, London 1988.

6. K. Hemmerle, *Thesen einer trinitarischen Ontologie*, Einsiedeln 1976.

7. G. Greshake, *Der dreieine Gott. Eine trinitarische Theologie*, Freiburg, Basel and Vienna 1997.

8. The conclusion presents readers with four types of artistic representations of the Trinity (three figures with the same form, the three visitors of Abraham, the seat of grace, the coronation of Mary by the Trinity), and seeks to sensitize them to its presence in music.

9. Note the deductive method of the author, which determines all these epistemological decisions. After briefly developing what he calls the 'basic experience' of the New Testament (pp.4–50), he devotes the whole of the first part to the immanent Trinity before moving on in the second part – again deductively (the trinitarian understanding of creation precedes the exposition of its dramatic form) – to the mysteries of Christianity and finally, in the third part, to the context of present-day societies.

10. See further C. Theobald, '"The Lord and Giver of Life". Towards a Theology of Life', *Concilium* 2000/1, pp.62–78.

11. Although the author notes in passing the need first of all to *relate* the event of revelation, ibid., p.48.

12. Cf. the formula on p.179, quoted above. Even contrary to his main witness H. Urs von Balthasar, the author dismisses the traditional problem of the 'trinitarian processions' (original relationships), which he attributes to a Western thought that is monopolized by the idea of unity (above all pp.192–95), in favour of his own conception of 'communion'. The effect of this decision is that the question of paternity (and generation) is passed over in silence in the anthropological discussions of sexuality and society. One sign of this is that Eph. 3.14ff. ('All fatherhood . . .') is not quoted once. Is this a trinitarian theology for 'a society without fathers'? Another indication which is not unconnected with what has gone before is that in the long discussion of the concept of person, the few pages on philosophy and social psychology (pp.165–68) ignore the problem of violence in the constitution of the 'person'. We might have expected that the 'method of correlation' would lead to a verification of the 'trinitarian key' of the first part. The debate should then relate both to the current anthropological context and to the analogy, not only between the human *communio* and the trinitarian *communio* but also and at the same time between the 'persons' of the Trinity.

13. Cf. above all his major article, 'Eine Diskussion über den trinitarischen Personbegriff. Karl Rahner und Bernd Jochen Hilberath', *ZKTh* 111, 1989, pp.129–62.

14. This ethical reference could provide the starting point for a theological reflection on the autonomy of creation, human history and the earth, which today prove to be autonomous, to the point of being able to bring out *in them* the

ultimate possibility of the human being, which is holiness.

15. Cf. C. Theobald, 'Der eine Gott und seine Zeugen. Zu einer Theologie der Begegnung zwischen Juden, Christen und Moslims', *Bijdragen* 58, 1997, pp.79–96.

# An Orthodox Approach to the Mystery of the Trinity: Questions for the Twenty-First Century

Orthodox theologians sometimes approach the trinitarian mystery from exclusively within their own tradition. They restrict their investigations to the classic formulations of the Cappadocians and their patristic successors, the definitions of the Seven Ecumenical Councils, the Byzantine controversies over the *filioque* and Palamism, and the views of more recent Orthodox theologians. Orthodox theology is always grounded in these sources, yet in practice it has always interacted with Western theology and culture as well. To understand the Orthodox tradition and continue its work, it is important to see how past and present Orthodox theologians have responded creatively to the burning issues of their times in dialogue with their contemporary cultures. This has been as true in the twentieth century as the fourth; it remains the case in the twenty-first century.

For about the last twenty-five years, there has been much interest in the Trinity among Western theologians, inspired at least in part by their encounters with the work of Orthodox theologians like Vladimir Lossky and John Zizioulas. Today Orthodox theologians face the challenge and the opportunity to engage in dialogue with these Westerners, since the questions they pose in re-examining classical trinitarian concepts are those of the contemporary global culture we all share. Our answers, faithful to our tradition, will frequently differ from theirs. This in turn can challenge them to further rethinking. The new context may also enable us to reframe in new ways our long-standing questions about such matters as the eternal relationship between the Son and the Spirit or the relationships among divine persons and energies and the created world. Such reflection may enable Eastern and Western theologians alike to move beyond old impasses.

## I. Three major themes

Twentieth-century discussions of the mystery of the Trinity have centered on three major themes that express concerns shared by theologians of the Eastern and the Western churches. Their reflections have often emerged through their fruitful dialogue with each other. They have sought to address many of the same questions, though often in different ways.

### 1. The concept of personhood

The first theme is personhood as a primary ontological category in our understanding of God and humankind. This concept is grounded in the Cappadocian understanding of the Trinity, which starts from the three hypostases rather than the common divine essence. Yet modern Orthodox theologians have developed their ideas of personhood in dialogue with nineteenth-century German idealism and twentieth-century existentialism. Moreover, the Orthodox do not have a monopoly on Christian personalism, which has also been a major theme in twentieth-century Western theology. It has come to dominate late twentieth-century Western trinitarian reflection. The other traditional concepts used in speaking of the Trinity, such as essence, energies, *perichoresis*, relations of origin, divine activity *ad extra*, etc., need to be re-articulated in ways that accord with contemporary understandings of personhood. Much of today's trinitarian reflection in East and West is engaged in this task.

### 2. Presence in the creation

The second theme asserts that the same relationality that links the divine persons with each other also extends from them to embrace humankind and all of creation. Theologians in the West have retrieved the biblical and patristic roots of trinitarian theology and have broken through the fossilized formulations that seemingly confined the relationality among the three persons within a self-enclosed divine realm so that created beings would have no access to the Trinity as Trinity. Although awareness of a trinitarian presence in creation was obscured in some 'scholasticized' Western triadology, opportunities for living encounter with the divine persons as persons have always continued to exist in the West, especially in contexts of worship and spirituality. Reaffirming the continued reality and importance of trinitarian contemplation and praxis in Christian life, Western theologians now regard Karl Rahner's principle that the immanent Trinity is the economic

Trinity and vice versa almost as axiomatic. It has become a starting point for further discussion. While the Eastern churches have always preserved a living awareness of the Trinity as present and active in creation and in human experience, we are faced with similar issues within our own tradition about how *theologia* is related to *oikonomia*. This point is central to discussions of the procession of the Holy Spirit and the essence-energies distinction. In both of these contexts, Orthodox theologians need to think more about how to affirm that the divine persons relate to the created world in ways that manifest and extend their eternal relationships with each other.

## 3. Trinity as interrelatedness

The third theme is the emphasis on the Trinity as community and as the source and model for community among humankind and in creation. In the West, liberation and feminist theologians see the equality and mutual interrelatedness and self-offering of the divine persons as providing the foundation for restructuring society in more just and inclusive ways. God as community challenges the hegemony of human authoritarianism and entrenched injustice. Moreover, God is perceived not as a distant monarch ruling the universe from afar but as a threefold presence encompassing the world within itself. Orthodox theologians also regard the Trinity as a model for the just society. Moreover, this concept enables the relationship between humankind as divine image and the created world to be reframed, so that the human vocation can be seen more as priestly cosmic mediation than as domination. Thus contemporary Eastern and Western theologians have in different ways adopted a 'panentheism' that addresses ecological concerns. Further thinking would be useful to clarify the theological and ethical implications of all these ideas.

The Orthodox belief that the Father is the source of God's being and unity has contemporary appeal because it produces an ontology grounded in a person rather than an 'impersonal' essence, but it also raises questions because it entails a hierarchical ordering, a *taxis* within the Trinity. For this reason, some Western theologians have discarded it altogether. Orthodox theologians have the task of articulating more clearly how hierarchy and community can coexist within the Godhead and consequently in humankind and creation without threatening the values of human and cosmic justice that have their source in the Trinity.

## II. Fatherhood and community

In the context of personhood, let us reflect briefly on the themes of fatherhood and community and then consider the immanent and economic relationality of the Trinity. According to Athanasius and the Cappadocians, God's fatherhood must not be understood as a projected image of human patriarchy. Rather, God as Father is the ultimate model for every human parent and leader in family, church and society (cf. Eph. 3.15). This has radical implications for the praxis of human family life and social hierarchy.

### *1. Mutual love*

God the Father begets the Son and breathes forth the Holy Spirit so as to endow them with everything he is. He gives them all his divinity, all his glory, all his creative power, all his authority. He lets them act on his behalf to create, sustain and perfect the universe. He allows the Son and the Spirit to represent him and make him known in the world. He does not keep anything for himself alone but shares everything he is and gives everything he has to them. Their greatness is what constitutes his glory as a Father.

As many twentieth-century theologians in East and West have observed, it is wrong to think that in the Trinity self-emptying and deference to other persons belong specifically to the Son and the Holy Spirit. The self-emptying which is particularly characteristic of the loving and humble God, like everything else, begins with the Father. The Son and the Spirit respond to his humble love by offering the same back to him, so their relationship is mutual. In John's Gospel we read that the Father has given the key divine attributes of glory and judgment to the Son, and yet the Son seeks only to glorify the Father and defer to his judgment. This character of mutual love, humility and self-offering, which has God the Father as its foundation with the Son and the Spirit, is what provides the model for human community.

### 2. *Divine* kenosis

Divine *kenosis* and suffering comprise another major theme of twentieth-century theology in East and West. We cannot address this topic adequately here, but a few remarks are in order. Some Russian thinkers, perhaps influenced by Hegel, have suggested that in eternity the Father negates himself and suffers in giving himself totally to the Son, so the life of the Trinity is inherently a tragedy. This opinion is based on a fundamental misunderstanding of personhood. If a person is constituted by its relatedness to other persons, the divine persons are fulfilled as persons, not negated, precisely in offering themselves to each other. Since God is love, their mutual *kenosis* is their eternal joy in glorifying each other. The life of the Trinity, which is perfect mutual love, cannot be a cause of suffering in God. Divine suffering must be a response to fallen creatures who reject God's love. Because of our sinfulness and the fallenness of the world, divine *kenosis* and self-offering are incarnated in the agony of the cross. Yet as through the resurrection death is swallowed up in the life of the Trinity, so also this torment, though it is too great for the world to contain, is ultimately dissolved in the joy of the Father, Son and Spirit. They ever delight in their mutual self-offering and in the salvation of the world, which they achieve by the outpouring of their own life.

People often need guidance and leadership from others. As they progress spiritually, Orthodox Christians become more and more aware of this; they recognize their interrelatedness and dependence on others and on God more and more clearly. In human life, situations arise continually in which some lead and others are led. Therefore, even when they are temporary and linked to specific and limited functions, hierarchical relationships naturally emerge in community. So Christ did not decree the abolition of hierarchy but instead instituted it and simultaneously mandated its inversion. The apostles are enthroned, but they must at the same time take the last place and become servants of all, as their Master did (cf. Luke 22.25–30). This pattern of human relationality is grounded directly in God the Father and the life of the Trinity. God does not despair of hierarchy or destroy it but transfigures it into equality, mutual interdependence and self-offering, that is genuine community. This is also our task as human persons created in God's image.

## III. Immanent Trinity and economic Trinity

The life the divine persons share with humankind and the created world must be the same life they share with each other, a life genuinely their own. Thus, their relationships with created beings must be understood as manifestations and extensions of their eternal relationships with each other. God created the world in love, with the aim of drawing it within the eternal triune life of love. This means that the divine persons cannot be thought to have one pattern of intra-divine relationality and another, radically different, pattern of relationality towards the created world. We cannot say, as Augustine did, that they relate to each other as three but to the world only as one. Thus the 'economic' Trinity revealed and known to human beings is truly the eternal 'immanent' Trinity.

## *1. Radical transcendence*

Contemporary Eastern and Western theologians generally agree on this. Yet when some Western theologians discard the concept of the immanent Trinity altogether and collapse it into the economic Trinity, Orthodox theologians find this problematic. In our tradition, it is essential to affirm God's radical transcendence. Although we may know God genuinely, we can never know God exhaustively, even in the age to come. As Gregory of Nyssa explains, since God is infinite and we as creatures are finite, by grace our capacity to receive divine life can expand indefinitely, but at any given point it remains limited. There is always more to God beyond what we can contain; some of this we will receive in the future, yet what lies beyond remains inexhaustible and surpasses all imagining. Thus, there must be some reality that the divine persons share with each other that we can never know, not because they jealously keep it for themselves but because we remain unable to receive it. Orthodox theology calls this the unknowable divine essence, or, more precisely, that which is beyond essence, since it escapes categorization in terms of any essentialist ontology. Yet we also affirm unequivocally that the Father, Son and Holy Spirit we know are the same persons who coexist eternally. The immanent Trinity is the economic Trinity in that the persons who comprise the Trinity are the same, and they are known and loved as the persons they genuinely are by redeemed humankind as well as by each other. They share their common life and mutual relationships with the creation freely. Yet there remains an 'immanent' dimension of their existence, an absolute transcendence that is uniquely their own.

## *2. Sharing in the life of the Trinity*

This transcendence, however, is not a barrier separating us from God. The three persons' relationships with us are truly extensions and manifestations of their relationships with each other. This follows from Gregory Palamas' statement that what is unknowable in the divine essence is revealed in the energies. The Trinity revealed in creation and the history of salvation is the same as the eternal Trinity. As the three persons work together to accomplish the salvation of the world, in the ways described in scripture, their activities follow the same patterns as their eternal interactions with each other. When the Father sends the Son and the Spirit into the world in the incarnation and at Pentecost, these temporal missions manifest and extend their eternal generation and procession from the Father. When the Son and the Spirit offer the world back to the Father, this manifests and extends their eternal offering of themselves to the Father. According to the classic pattern delineated by the Cappadocians and other patristic authors, the Father always acts in the created world through the Son in the Holy Spirit. All of God's creative and saving activity thus originates in the good will of the Father, is accomplished by the Son, and is perfected by the Spirit. Correspondingly, human persons approach and come to know God and participate in divine life in the opposite order. We come in the Holy Spirit through the Son to the Father. This fundamental structure of trinitarian relationality and activity in creation must also express the way the three persons are related to each other. We share in the life of the Trinity by being included in this specific structure of relationality. Orthodox theologians need to think further about how the procession of the Spirit from the Father and the Son's eternal relationship with the Spirit are situated within this overall structure.

Moreover, it is essential to affirm that when we participate in this structure of trinitarian relationality, within it we enter into direct, interpersonal relationships with each of the divine persons. While much of the Orthodox church's solemn liturgical worship is offered in the Holy Spirit through the Son to the Father, we also speak directly to each of the three in prayer. Many public prayers are addressed to Christ, and almost every service begins with a direct invocation of the Holy Spirit. In our personal prayers we can contemplate or speak freely to each of the three, entering into a dialogue of mutual love with each of them and all of them. As we come in the Spirit through the Son to the Father, we must not understand this to mean that the Father is farthest from us and the Spirit closest. Rather, all three are equally transcendent yet equally close and immediately present. As Boris Bobrinskoy observes, our relationship to the Father is direct and intimate; he is not a distant eminence we approach only indirectly. John 14.23 promises that the Father will dwell within those who are faithful to Christ's teachings in word and deed.

### 3. *Trinitarian* perichoresis

Our *lex credendi* must therefore be understood so as to allow for this interpersonal *lex orandi*. That is, our communion with God in the Spirit through the Son to the Father must be seen as establishing us in a place where we are freely related in divine love to each of the persons and can approach any and all of them, as it were, in every direction. All of them together, and each one distinctly, are immediately present to us and surround us in divine love. We find ourselves, as it were, *within* the Trinity's common activity *ad extra*, which is itself a threefold personal dynamism that encompasses the whole universe and all of history. The Father enables this through the Son in the Holy Spirit, yet within this fixed structure, loving relationality is spontaneous, dynamic, open and unlimited.

This freedom and openness in our relationship with the divine persons manifests and extends the eternal *perichoresis* of the Trinity, as God graciously shares with us God's interpersonal life. In their mutual love the three persons dwell eternally in each other and continually pass into and through each other. Each is present in the other two and offers himself to them, receiving them into himself. As Dumitru Staniloae has suggested, this mutual indwelling is dynamic, spontaneous and unlimited and overflows freely in every direction. Divine love cannot be restricted. So the fixed structure of the eternal trinitarian relationships, established in the generation of the Son and the procession of the Spirit from the Father, must be understood as constituting a space, as it were, in which their free interpersonal relationality occurs. Bobrinskoy, who emphasizes that their missions in history reveal what they are eternally, points towards the same conclusion by showing in detail how the collaborations among the three persons described in scripture follow a variety of different patterns. This free, collaborative activity of the Trinity in history is the point where we encounter the divine persons and are drawn through their love to share in their mutual *perichoresis*, which must thus be understood as extending into and encompassing the created world. More reflection is needed about how trinitarian *perichoresis* relates to the energies and activities of the three persons.

# The Nature of Biblical Monotheism: Experience and Ideology

MARK O'BRIEN

It is fair to say that contemporary biblical study is much more ideologically self-conscious than previous generations. In particular, it has become acutely aware of the subjective factor, the impact that a reader's stance has on the experience and understanding of the biblical text. What is driving current biblical research is of course vitally important for contemporary readers but it is not the only thing. In many ways, we are still running on the momentum generated by biblical study in the early church and the subsequent reactions to this pioneering study. To get some sense of the impact of the contemporary scene, it is worth taking a look at the earlier ones: they were informed by different ideologies and they offer the reader a different experience of the biblical text.[1]

## I. The problem: experience of God or self-centered constructions?

The early church's theology of inspiration was modelled closely on its understanding of prophecy. This fostered the conviction that, in reading the OT, one had direct access to Israel's experience of God, to God's word and to the way God intervened in human affairs. The church needed to explain its founder and itself in relation to the OT, the established sacred text. OT texts were scrutinized for prophecies that pointed to Jesus and/or the church; for stories that illustrated, even in an embryonic way, Christian themes. There were texts that did not seem to point in this direction, at least on an initial reading. Nevertheless, by imaginative use of typology and allegory, readers were able to argue that there was a deeper, hidden, meaning in these texts. This was their true meaning and it pointed to Jesus and the church.

In relation to monotheism, the biblical account was accepted as historically accurate. YHWH, the one God, was known to Israel's pre-diluvian ancestors and, after the flood, this same YHWH called Abraham and Sarah to be a blessing to all the families of the earth (Gen. 12.1–3). In reading and reflecting on the biblical account of Israel's relationship with God, Christians believed that God was also speaking to them. Typology and allegory bolstered this belief by portraying an OT that was pregnant with Christian meaning. In short, the theologies of the day aided the conviction that the OT provided immediate access for Christians to the experience of God.

The prospect of experiencing God directly in the scriptures has a powerful attraction and is no doubt a major reason why this approach continues to appeal. Human beings are innately self-centered: we become interested in God because we hope, at least in part, that there is something in it for us. In terms of what we might call raw appeal, the early church's ideology – which portrayed the biblical text as a medium for a direct and (presumably) positive experience of God – has a head start over more recent theories. For these, the access is not immediate: the relationship between reader, text, and author is more complex.

Later scholarship saw serious flaws in the inherited approach to the OT. It was accused of distorting the OT's understanding of God, of reshaping it to make it fit for Christian consumption. In reply, the church could argue that the guidance of the Holy Spirit ensured a true and authentic understanding. In the eyes of the critics, however, the church's use of typological and allegorical exegesis so loaded the texts with Christian meaning that it impeded an accurate appreciation of the God portrayed in these texts. The ideology may have claimed to illuminate the real meaning of OT texts; in reality, it clouded their meaning.

If anything, the accusation and likely reply signals the importance of the subjective factor – how the reader sees it. Surprisingly, the historical critical analysis that came to dominate study of the OT in the West until recently did not focus on the reader. Instead, it launched a scientific, objective project to rescue the OT from the 'control' of the church and to allow its authentic voice to be heard. It may not have intended to do so at the outset, but the rescue effort came to have a profound impact on how the Bible is understood, both as a record of God's dealings with Israel and as the Word of God.

## II. Monotheism as a product of catastrophe and defeat

Critical study effectively opened a gap between the history of Israel as 'reconstructed' by scholars and the 'history' recounted in the text of the OT. In a host of areas, the two did not tally. With respect to monotheism, the OT tells how Israel deviated from its foundational commitment to the one God and strayed into polytheism. According to critical analysis, Israel probably began as a polytheistic society – like other ancient Near Eastern societies – and developed its theology of monotheism only after a prolonged struggle led by parties who promoted devotion to the god YHWH. The exile in 587 BCE marked a watershed in the rise of monotheism, with second-Isaiah its principal advocate (cf. Isa. 45).[2] Faced with this gap between text and history, readers either had to abandon belief in the Bible as the Word of God or reassess its nature and purpose. A way forward was to focus attention on the biblical authors themselves, to view them as creative theologians and their texts as theological discourses rather than historical records.

According to this understanding, the biblical text does not provide immediate access to Israel's experience of God as the early church assumed. But, it does enable a reader to reflect on Israel's theologizing about God and to do so for different stages in the composition of a text. For example, historical analysis pointed to Deut. 32.8–9 as evidence of early Israelite polytheism. YHWH is one among the gods and YHWH's portion, as distributed by the 'Most High', is the people of Jacob. If this interpretation is accurate, it implies that the theologian who composed these verses had a radically different understanding of God from the monotheistic theology that dominates the present text.[3] Passages such as Num. 25, Hosea 9.10, and Ps. 106.28 were also tabled as evidence of polytheism: their hostility to the worship of other gods betrays its actual practice.

Given that early Israel was polytheistic, what motivated the later decisive move to monotheism? Was it a desire to cover up an earlier embarrassing theology? Given the OT's relentless critique of Israel and its relationship with God, this seems unlikely. Besides, if the present text is a cover-up job, why leave traces of polytheism in it? OT editors seem too careful to make such slip-ups. Another possible reason is that Israel had a dramatic experience that stimulated a major revision of its theology. For many historical critics, this experience was the exile in 587 BCE. The impact of the exile was so decisive for monotheistic theology and its proclamation became so important that the editors of the OT decided to begin their story with it. Polytheistic texts, such as Deut. 32.8–9, may have been retained out of respect for (ancient) tradition or because they could be read (allegorically?) in a monotheistic way.

According to this hypothesis, belief in one all-powerful God is the product of catastrophe and defeat, not triumph and success – an astonishing leap of faith.[4] Unfortunately, the complexity of the texts, their multi-layered nature, and critical reflection on the relationship between experience and ideology do not instil confidence that one can name the experience that gave monotheism the decisive edge. Against the above hypothesis, it could be argued that monotheistic theologians just did their job better than the others, or that monotheism became the ideology of the ruling class in the post-exilic period – and history is written by the winners. Each of these possibilities should, in principle, be acceptable to a believer in divine inspiration. As the saying goes, God works in strange ways.

## III. The challenge of synchronic analysis: making decisions

Whichever hypothesis among the above is favoured, one thing is clear and shared by all: historical critical analysis signals a profound change in the way the text is perceived. Whereas the early church thought of itself as listening to God's words in the text of the OT, the critically aware reader listens to the words of Israel's theologians in the text of the OT. There is evocative power in the portrait of Israel 'discovering' monotheism in the chaos of the exile, but it provides a different experience from that of a reader in the early church because of the different ideology informing it.

Historical, or diachronic, analysis sought to facilitate the reading of the OT as OT. The attempt has received mixed reviews. For some, it has been successful: for others, it seems the understanding of the divinity is more ancient Near Eastern than specifically OT.[5] There has been a tendency in some quarters of historical analysis to see ancient Israelites as ciphers of ancient Near Eastern thought rather than creative, imaginative authors in their own right. A theology of inspiration need not have problems with this viewpoint but, given recent research on biblical literature, a low assessment of Israelite creativity seems unjustified.[6]

Despite recent negative evaluation, historical analysis remains a significant force in contemporary biblical study.[7] It does, after all, challenge a reader to consider the situation out of which a text emerged and to which it was addressed. Nevertheless, this approach now has to reckon with rivals that are of considerable import for one's appreciation of biblical monotheism. Among these are discourse-oriented or synchronic analysis – in many ways a critical reaction to the perceived shortcomings of diachronic or historical analysis – deconstruction theory, and the hermeneutics of suspicion. Associated with the hermeneutics of suspicion are various emancipatory or advocacy projects such as feminist criticism, liberation theology and post-colonial theology.

Synchronic analysis concedes the possibility that Israel worshipped other gods at some stage in its history but argues that this is not what the OT presents. In the present text, worship of other gods is consistently condemned. Names such as Elyon and El Shaddai may once have been the names of other gods but this is not their function in the present text: here they refer to YHWH (e.g., Gen. 14.18–20; 17.1; 35.11). Synchronic analysis does not believe there is any profit in trying to uncover the processes by which such names came to be applied to YHWH. The textual basis is too small and the results are too speculative. Such 'excavative' analysis goes against the grain of the text.

This may look reassuring to those who seek a unified OT. Where synchronic analysis begins to chafe and challenge is in its notions of characterization and point of view. YHWH, like Adam and Eve, is a character in the story of Gen. 2–3. The reader is invited to view the characters in the story as one views portraits in a gallery. The portraits may draw on tradition or personal experience but they have been 'created' for this story. Within the larger OT gallery, there is a great, and challenging, variety of portraits of YHWH the one God. The variety is so extensive and the differences so marked that any claim to have grasped 'the' OT undertanding of monotheism must be viewed with caution.

To give some examples. I Sam. 15.29 proclaims that God's mind does not change, unlike a man's. Judg. 10.13 and 16, on the other hand, indicate that God's mind does change. Between II Kings 10.30 and Hosea 1.4, God's mind changes quite radically in relation to the house of Jehu. In Joshua, God is a warrior bent on destruction of Israel's enemies; in Isa. 19.24–25, God is a peacemaker who bestows blessings on Israel's (former) enemies. In Gen. 1, God in sublime transcendance creates by pronouncing a word. In Job 38–41 and Ps. 89.10–11, God battles the forces of chaos to bring about the order of creation.[8]

A particularly striking case is Ex. 34.6–7 where contradictory attitudes are attributed to God within the space of a verse. In one view, God is 'gracious and merciful, slow to anger . . . forgiving iniquity and transgression and sin'. In the other, God by no means clears the guilty, 'visiting the iniquity of the parents upon the children . . . to the third and fourth generation'. The narrative does not resolve this tension; the texts are simply juxtaposed. According to synchronic analysis, the reader must, initially at least, give equal weight to the two points of view. The tension cannot be resolved by recourse to allegory or history. Examination of the text signals in the immediate and more remote context may indicate the OT favours one view over the other. But this kind of examination is fraught with difficulty, not only because of the amount of evidence to be sifted but also because of factors influencing the reader, whether an individual or a church community. In the end I believe, a reader or readers is drawn to ask questions and make decisions about the nature of the biblical text and about the value of the text.

About the nature of the text. Does it impose thought or invite the reader to think? Is Ex. 34.6–7 imposing both views or inviting the reader to consider each and make a decision? Analysis of the larger OT may help in making a decision but it is unlikely to relieve one of the need to make a decision. The 'correct" view will not simply fall out of the Bible after x-amount of analysis. The OT is too subtle for that and too keen to engage the reader in theological dialogue.

About the value of the text. A reader will at some stage have to make a decision about which text gives meaning and authenticity to his or her life. Some may see meaning in the notion that the one God can abound both in steadfast love of sinners and in steadfast punishment of sinners. It is likely, however, that most will decide one view is acceptable and the other is not. Personal factors will play an important role in this decision.

## IV. Shifting portrayals of God

But, to make a decision is not the end of the matter. The unacceptable view does not disappear but remains as a disturbing presence in the biblical text. Moreover, as one attempts to come to grips with the larger OT and NT, the shifting portrayals of God create an impression of a text that is unable to draw a definitive outline of God or resists the temptation to do so. It invites one to look and ponder but it does not (or cannot) say in the end who or what God is. The ideology most closely associated with this phenomenon in the biblical text is deconstructionism. The phenomemon is, of course, not unique to the Bible. Deconstructive analysis calls for renewed reflection about how the biblical text shapes one's understanding and experience of God. It also challenges any claim to provide a unified account of biblical monotheism: the theory requires not only the text itself to be deconstructed but also one's interpretation of it.

Synchronic analysis has seen a marked shift in interest from the author of a text to the reader of the text – witness the above references to the reader. The reader is now seen more as a maker of meaning than a passive recipient of meaning. The impact of this on one's experience of the God of the OT is quite different from that of historical analysis. According to the latter the reader can reconstruct the various processes by which Israel's theologians reflected on their experience of God (e.g, I Kings 8). According to the former we are not able to reconstruct these processes. What we can observe is how the reader 'constructs' the portrait of God from the signals in the text and the impact that this has on the reader (e.g. in the book of Jonah).

The focus on the reader invites some comment on the hermeneutics of suspicion. This approach argues that texts and their readers are biased in ways that tend to go unacknowledged. The parade example here is the male bias of the Bible and, until recently, of most academic study associated with it. To put it another way, any reading of the Bible has a streak of advocacy in it. According to the hermeneutics of suspicion, study of the Bible can only be responsible and accountable when bias in the text and its readers is exposed and acknowledged. For its part, advocacy analysis sees legitimacy in the inevitable bias of our reading, if it is handled in a critical and accountable way. Thus, a feminist or liberationist approach to the text, when applied and assessed critically, allows one to see things that can be obscured by other readings.

Once one becomes aware of bias in the Bible, it can have significant impact on one's understanding of its authority and on how it mediates the experience of God. The predominantly male images of God, for example, create a negative and offensive experience for many readers. Nevertheless, when handled critically, this bias in the biblical text can be seen in a less negative light. It challenges readers to fill in what is seen to be lacking in the Bible. It is also a reminder that human beings never escape the subjective factor and therefore have a limited ability to communicate experience effectively, whether they be biblical authors or critical readers. In Paul's words, 'now we see in a mirror dimly' (I Cor. 13.12).

Interestingly, advocacy analysis turns one's thoughts again to the exegesis practised by the early church. A Christian reading of the OT is, in a sense, a form of advocacy analysis. Too much ideology has flowed under the bridge for a critically informed reader simply to return to the early church's practice. Nevertheless, a Christian approach to the OT, employing typology and allegory in a critical and accountable way, may channel readers into new experiences of the text and its proclamations about God.

## Notes

1. For reasons of space, the focus throughout will be on the OT.
2. An accessible version of this viewpoint was outlined by B. Lang in *Monotheism and the Prophetic Minority* (The Social World of Biblical Antiquity Series, 1), Sheffield: The Almond Press 1983, pp.13–60.
3. This interpretation of Deut. 32.8–9 depends on reading 'sons of God' (or 'gods') where the Hebrew has 'sons of Israel'. For a discussion of the difficulties, see A. D. H. Mayes, *Deuteronomy* (NCB), Grand Rapids: Eerdmans 1979, pp. 384–85.
4. Here, the 'Suffering Servant' passages in Isa. 42.1–4 (5–9); 49.1–7; 50.4–9 and 52.13–53.12 come to mind.
5. For a recent discussion of how much ancient Near Eastern thought shaped the OT, see the relevant contributions in W. Dietrich and M. A. Klopfenstein (eds), *Ein Gott Allein? JHWH-Verehrung und biblischer Monotheismus im Kontext der israelitischen und altorientalischen Religionsgeschichte* (OBO 139), Göttingen: Vandenhoeck & Ruprecht 1994.
6. See, for example, R. Alter, *The Art of Biblical Literature*, New York: Basic Books 1981.
7. For example, L. G. Perdue believes historical analysis is moribund; see *The Collapse of History* (OBT), Minneapolis: Fortress Press 1994.
8. The whole question of how God is portrayed in the OT prophetic books is too complex to enter into here.

# God as Experience and Mystery: The Early Christian Understanding

SEÁN FREYNE

## I. Between immanence and transcendence of God

Early Christian theological speculation occurs at the intersection of Jewish belief in one God and Graeco-Roman speculation about the nature of the divine and its interaction with the world of humans. Indeed this encounter between Jewish monotheism and Graeco-Roman paganism had already taken place among Hellenistic Jewish writers, and is represented best in the writings of Philo of Alexandria, and to a lesser extent Josephus, both of whom are first-century CE figures, contemporaneous with the rise and spread of Christianity. These Graeco-Jewish writers had sought to explain their faith in 'one God' in ways that met the exigencies of Greek philosophy and apologetic discussion without dissolving it into the tolerant monotheism of the times represented by the slogan 'God is both one and many'.

Two aspects emerge as highly significant, aspects that are in some tension with each other. On the one hand the mysterious nature of God was central to Jewish thought from the episode at the burning bush: God refuses to give his name but assures Moses that he would be with Israel in its desert wanderings. Thus the second command of the decalogue prohibits any graven images of God who is deemed to be beyond any form of human representation. Yet, this God can equally be described anthropomorphically as having walked with Adam and Eve in Paradise 'in the cool of the evening' (Gen. 2). This sense of God's nearness never deserted Israel: God was the God of history, present to Israel in the desert wanderings, the conquest of the land, the Babylonian exile, or the return to Zion.

### *1. 'The Lord your God is one . . .'*

The Jewish tradition, be it in the homeland or the diaspora, was always concerned therefore with the tension between the immanence and the

transcendence of God, so central to its scriptural heritage, but without compromising the principle of only one God, enshrined in the daily prayer of all
Jews: Hear O Israel, the Lord your God is one. Graeco-Roman paganism
on the other hand has traditionally been described as polytheistic, since the
traditional pantheon consisted of various identifications of the divine in
terms of natural forces, such as sea, wind, sky, water, fire etc. The various
myths or stories about the origins and exploits of these gods had continued
to be commented on and interpreted throughout the centuries prior to the
emergence of Christianity. Increasingly, philosophers tended to be critical
of the immorality and amorality of the gods. Thus the stereotype of paganism as essentially polytheistic is coming to be revised. God is both one and
many, and the various images of the gods are merely different ways of representing the one divine reality that controls the universe and is at its very
heart. Philo, the Jewish Alexandrian philosopher, is to be understood in this
context, drawing on ideas that were current in middle Platonism. According
to this tradition the Supreme God can only be known through philosophical
speculation and was not, therefore, accessible to the masses. According to
Philo, this is the unnamed God of the Israelite tradition. The various
anthropomorphisms for God in the Hebrew Bible on the other hand
referred to the Demiurge or creator God whom the philosophers regarded as
distinct from the Supreme God, whose nature it was 'not to be named, but
to be' (Philo, *On Dreams* l, pp.230–33).

The rabbinic scholars were less concerned with the philosophical tradition than with interpreting the scriptural witness within the emerging
system of orthodoxy which they sought to establish. The tradition of speaking about God in such images as king, shepherd, teacher, judge, warrior and
the like was extended in the later books of the Bible, particularly through the
figure of personified wisdom who was deemed to be separate from God but
which still acted as a partner in creation (Prov. 8.22–31). Other personifica-
tions of God of a more impersonal kind were also developed in terms of
God's name (*memra*), God's glory (*chabod*) and God's presence (*shekinah*),
in order to avoid any dissolution of God's transcendence, but also to avert
the dangers of more crass anthropomorphism.

Both the philosophical and exegetical efforts to preserve the distinctive
Hebraic notion of 'one God alone' were not without their difficulties, however. Philo's acceptance of the distinction between the Supreme God and
the Demiurge, both fostered an élitism that was not part of the Israelite
conception of election and also hinted at an oppositional dualism between
pure spirit that is good and matter that is evil, as was fully developed in later

Gnostic systems. Again this was a conception of God that was totally foreign to the Israelite tradition, no matter how mysterious God's true being might ultimately remain. Equally, the distinction between God and God's emanations (name, glory, presence etc.) could easily give rise to speculation about two powers in heaven, a doctrine condemned by the rabbis, because of the possible confusion with pagan mythological conceptions of the gods engaged in power struggles in heaven. A late rabbinic treatise declares: 'Scripture could not give an opportunity to the nations of the world that there were two powers in heaven, but declares: I am Yahweh your God. I was in Egypt, I was at the sea, I was in the past, I will be in the future to come; I am in this world and in the world to come' (Mekhilta de Rabbi Ishmael).

The reference to the nations of the world may well allude to the Christian understanding of God which had evolved from the New Testament scriptures, giving rise to the formulations of the councils of Nicea (325) and Chalcedon (451) on the unity and trinity of God. In the earlier period, however, Christian ideas about God were still part of the on-going Jewish debate, participating in both the philosophical and exegetical currents just mentioned. There was of course now a new factor that differentiated the early Christians from other branches of the parent religion, namely, the memory of Jesus and the present experience of him as the Risen One whose spirit was highly active in their community life. Thus it can be said that all early Christian *theo*logy should be described as *christ*ology. This insight calls for further elucidation. In the Christian experience the transcendence of God was indeed maintained fully, but the more Jesus' status was conceived in divine terms and proclaimed, the more God's immanence came to be acknowledged in the history of one individual's life and death. It is this element of 'double exposure' that makes the Gospels such unique documents, at once faith-inspired records of Jesus' earthly life and witnesses to Christian understanding of his true identity with and in God.

## 2. The Pauline letters

We can trace the first stages of this development in the Pauline letters which pre-date the Gospels by several decades. In some fragments of early Christian hymns which are embedded in various letters, the process described slightly later by the pagan writer Pliny – 'singing hymns to Christ as to a God' – shows an acquaintance with the philosophical language of the time. Jesus is described as being in the 'likeness' (*morphe*) of God before his earthly appearance, and after his self-emptying obedience he is graced with a name that is 'above every name', so that all should bow in homage before it (Phil. 2.6–11). This name is specified as 'Lord' (*kyrios*), the term that is invariably used in the Greek translation of the Bible (the LXX) for Yahweh. However, as is well known, Yahweh is not really a name for God, but is derived rather from the Hebrew version of God's promise to Moses at the burning bush: 'I will be with you' (Ex. 3.14). Thus in early Christian experience Jesus is endowed with the same quality as the Hebrew God, who despite his nearness to humans, is ultimately beyond naming or representation. This 'theology of the name' occurs in the post-Pauline Letter to the Hebrews also. Here the author seeks to counter speculation about Jesus that we know occurred in other contexts of Jewish thought of the period, especially at Qumran, dealing with the notion of angels representing the divine within the world. As befits the status of him who can be described as being the very expression of God's being, Jesus is said to have inherited a name far superior to that of the angels, heavenly beings though they may be (Heb. 1.1–4).

One can see traces of the exegetical trajectory also at work in the early Christian texts. The Markan Jesus responds to the address 'good master' by recalling the Jewish *Shema* : 'Why do you call me good? Nobody is good except God alone' (Mark 10.18; Deut. 6.4). The apparent distancing of Jesus from God (cf. also Mark 13.30) plays a role in Mark's theology as we shall presently discuss, but it is important to see how central the *Shema* was to early Christian thinking even prior to Mark. Writing to the Corinthians Paul presumes that his converts were familiar with the Jewish prayer, and that it has played an important part in developing their thinking about Jesus and his relationship with God. The passage deserves to be cited in full:

> Hence, as to the eating of food offered to idols, we know that 'no idol in the world really exists' and that 'there is no God but one'. Indeed, even though there may be so-called gods in heaven or on earth – as in fact there are many gods and many lords – yet for us there is one God, the Father, from whom are all things and for whom we exist, and one Lord, Jesus Christ, through whom are all things and through whom we exist (I Cor. 8.4–6).

Thus the structure of the Jewish *Shema* is maintained but it is suitably adapted to include Jesus within its orbit. The epithet 'Father' (Abba) is now applied to God and the term Lord of the original is given to Jesus, corresponding to early Christian hymnic usage, as we have seen. Furthermore, the notion of creation is introduced, but in terms that reflect Hellenistic debates about the causes of things: God is the originating cause ('*from* whom all things exist') and Jesus is the instrumental cause *('through* whom all things exist').

## II. God's revealed hiddenness

These examples must suffice to show how early Christian reflections on Jesus Christ were developed within the Jewish matrix of discussion about God's action in the world and God's transcendence of all created reality. The identification of Jesus with the many different expressions of God's expected emissary according to Jewish hopes – messiah, son of Man, son of God – helped to dilute to some extent the tension between God's total otherness and God's immanence. What was utterly new was that Jesus, the Galilean prophet, was identified as that expected one, thereby giving a very concrete response to the age-old question of God's agency and accessibility within the world. At the same time, early Christian experience, despite its faith claims about Jesus, continued to maintain God's total otherness in line with its Jewish inheritance. The eschatological and apocalyptic milieu of early Christian experience provided one avenue of resolution to the dilemma caused to its theology by its belief in Jesus. The memory of Jesus' presence in the past, his words and actions, pointed forward towards their future fulfilment in the final stage of the eschatological drama, now unfolding when 'God would be all in all' (I Cor. 15.28). However, another dimension was to reflect on the mysterious nature of Jesus' own earthly identity, as this came to narrative expression in the Gospels. The two modes of existence which Paul could describe in terms of flesh/spirit and earthly/heavenly dualities now provide the framework within which the narratives about Jesus become suffused with the presence of the Risen and glorified one who shares in the mysterious reality of God. In this regard the Gospels of Mark and John provide an intriguing contrast *and* convergence in dealing with the mystery of God's revealed hiddenness, which is the paradox at the heart of the Jewish and Christian scriptures. Each work will be examined separately from this point of view.

### *1. Mark and the mysterious messiah*

The author of Mark's Gospel has constructed a narrative that demands subtlety from its readers. 'Let the reader understand' (Mark 13.21) is directed not just to the reading of the 'little apocalypse' (ch. 13) but to the whole work with the aura of mystery and paradox which pervades the narrative from start to finish. The author's strategy is to provoke readers to explore beneath the surface of things, and discover for themselves the real story that is unfolding in the career of Jesus. It is not just Peter but all would-be ideal readers/disciples who can be chided for 'thinking the thoughts of men, not the thoughts of God' (Mark 8.33). To this end the reactions of all the characters to the narrated episodes – fear, bewilderment, misunderstanding, hostility – are intended to play on the reader's own emotions, and in the process hopefully lead them across the threshold of faith. 'Seeing' becomes the single most important metaphor for the understanding that it is hoped to generate, yet all too often the expected vision is lacking, most notably among the inner core circle of disciples who were specially chosen (Mark 3.13–19; 8.14–21).

The central, 'bread section' is particularly noteworthy in this regard, stitched together, as it is, with allusions to bread, granting of sight, hearing and understanding. After the first feeding miracle in the wilderness, an event full of resonances of Israel being accompanied by the divine presence in its desert wanderings, the disciples are sent away to the other side in the boat. In the midst of the ensuing storm Jesus appears to them but they do not recognize him, thinking that he was a ghost. At the end of the episode, when calm is restored to the sea and the troubled disciples, the evangelist/author gives us the sharp, critical comment: 'They did not understand concerning the bread, their hearts were hardened' (Mark 6.31). 'The bread' that should have disclosed Jesus' true identity points backwards to the manna of the desert wanderings, and forwards to the eucharistic bread of early Christian celebration. Both are signs of God's saving presence in the desert and in the life of the threatened Christian community, a presence that is concretized for ever in early Christian imagination and experience in the person of Jesus appearing to the stricken disciples on the Sea of Galilee. Similarly, after the second feeding miracle (8.1–10) a similar lack of understanding on the part of the disciples gives rise to a series of challenging questions from Jesus: 'Why do you debate that you have no bread? Do you not yet perceive nor understand? Having eyes do you not see and having ears do you not hear? And do you not remember?' . . . And he said to them, 'Do you not yet understand?'

Eyes to see clearly and ears to hear plainly are required by the disciples if they are to really understand the mystery unfolding among them. That such transformation is possible for those who seek it is illustrated by Mark in the stories of healing deaf and blind individuals which bracket this encounter with the disciples (Mark 7.31–37; 8.22–26). Shortly after this artfully crafted section, Peter as spokesperson for the disciples proclaims Jesus to be the Christ. When, however, he objects to Jesus' acceptance of the consequences of this title by heading for opposition in Jerusalem, he is chided for 'thinking the thoughts of men, not the thoughts of God'. Obviously Peter's eyes have not been fully opened to understand the paradoxical nature of the events unfolding before him. In contrast to Peter's partial blindness there is the case of the blind Bar Timaeus outside Jericho, who on receiving the gift of sight from Jesus, follows him enthusiastically on the way that leads to Jerusalem. In addition to this 'outsider' there is also the Roman centurion who at the foot of the cross confesses Jesus as the Son of God, seeing that 'thus he breathed his last' (15.39). Thus, 'seeing' for Mark means looking beyond the externals of events, and understanding their deeper significance in terms of God's expected intervention in the world of humans by discerning that that presence does not conform to everyday expectations and projections.

Mark's parable chapter (ch. 4) gives the clue to the source of his theological insights. Here he has collected three 'nature parables', stories told by Jesus about growth in the natural world and its significance for understanding God's ways in the world. The different types of soil are illustrative of human success and failure in discerning the mysterious presence of God; the smallness of the seed that is sown is in stark contrast to the greatness of the end result, and the mysterious nature of the growth process indicates that humans can neither influence nor understand God's ways, yet must be reassured that those ways are gift-laden for humans. Around these stories Mark has built a framework illustrating his theory of understanding God's presence in the career of Jesus, and the difficulty of understanding this which the disciples (and we as readers) encounter as the narrative unfolds. Parables can so easily become riddles, blocking rather than disclosing its paradoxical meaning. Yet understanding *one* parable can lead to the insight that makes sense of the total drama. Disclosive moments are rare. Yet when they do occur it is often in and through the mundane that they are experienced and then they can suffice for a lifetime of meaning and commitment, despite all the counter signs that life brings.

## 2. John's revelatory signs

Mark's drama unfolds gradually because its starting point lies within the everyday world of people and nature. From the outset John's meditative soliloquy addresses us 'from above', however. The historical Jesus of the Markan narrative is identified with the *Logos*/Word who has had a prior history with God. The reader, like the disciples, is presented with an *epiphania* of the divine glory which no longer resides in the Jerusalem temple, there to be accessed on the great feasts of the Jews, but in the encounter with Jesus, whose life symbolizes the spiritual nourishment that those feasts represent (water, wine, bread, light). However, this encounter is like that of Moses, a veiled encounter, calling for seeing, perception, understanding, and believing, and above all loving, a disposition to see beyond the externals and to understand the deeds of Jesus for what they truly are, signs of his Father's glory that resides in him. Thus, despite its very different starting point that might appear to destroy the veil that hides the divinity from the very start, John is close to Mark in his thinking about the divine-human encounter. True to his Jewish roots, even when he might be accused of being anti-Jewish, God is both near and hidden in the Johannine scheme of things also.

Let us begin with the encounter from the divine side. The statement of 1.14 that 'the Word became flesh and pitched his tent in our midst' already strikes an Exodus note of Yahweh's dwelling in the 'tent of meeting' in the desert wanderings of Israel. From this opening identification of Jesus' presence replicating the divine presence, the author's 'high' christology serves to underpin the reality of the divine revelation manifested in the career of Jesus. Time and again the unique union between Jesus and the Father is stressed. 'My Father works until now and I work,' Jesus declares in a reference to the creation story, as a way of justifying his own healings on the sabbath. He shares the Father's name (5.43; 17.11), has power over all things (3.35; 13.3) and has life in himself as the Father has (5.26), but without being open to the charge of being 'a second God'. His status is based on the complete union between Father and Son expressed in terms of mutual indwelling and mutual love (10.38; 14. 10f.; 17.21–23). Hence Jesus' actions are really the actions of the Father who dwells in him 'who does the works' (14.10). From the point of view of the author, Jesus' actions are an expression of God's creative power which continues to be operative – his works – yet at another level they are not self-explanatory, but serve rather as signs which the truly discerning can identify as manifestations of the divine glory.

The implied author becomes the plural 'we', embracing both disciples then and later: 'We saw his glory, the glory of the only-begotten of the Father, full of grace and truth.' Unlike the Markan disciples, the Johannine circle rarely waver from this stance expressed emphatically after the first Cana miracle: 'He revealed his glory and his disciples believed in him' (2.11). Despite this blinding experience, there is no compulsion or inevitability about the disciples' or any other person's acceptance of the epiphany of divine glory that is the encounter with Jesus. After the Jewish crowds abandon him for his 'hard saying', Jesus himself puts the question to the disciples: 'Will you also go away?' To which Peter, as spokespereson for the group, replies: 'Lord, to whom shall we go? You have the words of eternal life, and we have believed and have come to know that you are the holy one of God' (6.67–69). At the very end of the Gospel the same structure of the Johannine epiphanic experience is acknowledged, though now extended beyond the immediate circle of his followers. Thomas requires physical evidence before confessing the Risen Christ as his Lord and God, and Jesus allows this, while proclaiming as blessed also those 'who have not seen but have believed' (20.20).

This final statement looks beyond the immediate experience of eye-witnesses to a faith based on the word of others. Yet that proclamation is no mere human word in the Johannine perspective. Rather it is based on the Paraclete or Spirit of Truth which comes as a gift from the Father, and is promised as a permanent presence to the disciples by the departing Jesus in his farewell meeting with them (14.16f; 16.13). The Johannine faith experience is, then, a gift received that transforms the receiver into the giver. God is defined as love as well as light, and those who accept the revelation are transformed by it. 'Love one another as I have loved you' (15.12) and 'If we walk in the light as he is in the light, we have fellowship with one another' (I John 1.7). Thus, there is an ethical as well as a mystical aspect to the experience. Indeed it is only in the effort to replicate God's act of unconditional love that it is possible for the true union with God to occur (cf. I John 4.13–21).

The various Johannine dialogues (e.g. chs 4 and 9) are excellent examples of how the faith experience occurs within the Johannine ethos. In both instances the dialogue is generated from an initial encounter that leads to a preliminary naming of Jesus, as messiah or healer. However, this is merely the first stage on the journey to full-blown Johannine faith. Misunderstandings can lead to further illumination through the statements of Jesus which function as an in-depth commentary on the actions just performed.

Alternatively, they can also lead to the blinding of those who refuse to take the initial step and cannot therefore be drawn into the deeper exploration of Jesus' true identity. It is this openness to the gift of the encounter that eventually generates the trusting acceptance of Jesus as the ultimate revelation of God. There is deep if tragic irony at work here, in that those who refuse the invitation (the Jews, the Pharisees, the world, as representative figures) think they know in advance who Jesus is, either because of his place of origin or their 'superior' knowledge of how God's plan is supposed to operate. Their religious élitism or their rootedness to 'below' blocks the possibility for a true encounter. There is a strong ethical note in describing the failure of some to accept the light that is in their midst. Their works are evil (3.19), they have neither the word nor the love of God in them (5.38, 42), they judge according to the flesh (8.15), they are of the world or from below (8.23), they cannot bear to hear the words of Jesus because they are of their father, the devil (8.43f.), they do not know God (8.55), they have preferred the praise (*doxa*) of men to the glory (*doxa*) of God (12.43). By contrast 'everyone who is *of* (the pregnant *ek* of source and origin) the truth hears my voice' (18.36).

## Conclusion

Despite the fact that Mark and John represent two opposite poles of early Christian reflection on Jesus – the one from below, the other from above – both have a similar perspective on how the encounter with Jesus functioned in the life and faith of the first followers. Their conviction about the ultimate significance of Jesus' life did not come as a blinding flash that could not be ignored, but rather as a veiled revelation which demanded engagement, trust and commitment. Both the messianic secret of Mark and John's theology of signs are grounded in the Jewish experience of the hidden God who is very near. The more Christian reflection about Jesus' life was developed along the lines of transferring images for God from the Hebrew scriptures to him and his actions, the more clearly we can see this theological reserve at work. The fact that those images are so many and varied, often rooted in the ecological, historical and social experiences of Israel, means that God's ultimately mysterious nature was maintained, despite the sense of intimacy and partnership between Yahweh and Israel that is expressed in the various writings. Familiarity and awe are intertwined as the correct responses to God's favour to Israel. For John, knowing God is no mere intellectual experience, but rather being drawn into the mystery of God's life and love, as Jesus repeatedly emphasizes in the farewell discourses that are meant to define Christian existence within the world after his departure (chs 13–17).

Early Christian experience of Jesus as the ultimate expression of God's care would appear to have torn open the veil that kept the God of Israel from view (Mark 15.38). Yet, even then, the historical particularity of Jesus' life and work raises other questions about God's presence and activity within the whole of creation. In Jesus Christians do indeed have a definite pointer to the nature of God, so profoundly articulated in the statement 'God is love' (I John 4.16). This conclusion was not arrived at by any abstract speculation but rather by the genuine experience and memory of one who was love and care personified within the limited contours of his life and times. Yet the paradox at the heart of the Christian experience of God is that such a one had to die to meet the demands of unconditional love. God indeed remains the ultimate mystery, but sufficient has been experienced to make possible the eschatological declaration that in the end 'God will be all in all' (I Cor. 15.28).

## Further reading

J. Ashton, *Understanding the Fourth Gospel*, Oxford: Clarendon Press 1991.

P. Athanassiadi and M. Frede (eds), *Pagan Monotheism in Late Antiquity*, Oxford: Clarendon Press 2000.

J.M Byrne (ed), *The Christian Understanding of God Today*, Dublin: Columba Press 1993.

L. Hurtado, *One God, One Lord. Early Christian Devotion and Jewish Monotheism*, London: SCM Press 1988.

B. F. Meyer, *The Early Christians. Their World Mission and Self Discovery*, Wilmington, Del: Michael Glazier 1986.

J. Neusner (ed), *Judaic Perspectives on Ancient Judaism*, Philadelphia: Fortress Press 1987.

A. Segal, *Two Powers in Heaven. Early Rabbinic Reports about Christianity and Gosticism*, Leiden: Brill 1977.

W. Telford (ed), *The Interpretation of Mark*, Edinburgh: T. and T. Clark, 2nd edn 1995.

# The One God of Islam and Trinitarian Monotheism

CLAUDE GEFFRÉ

On 19 August 1986, addressing young Moroccans gathered in Casablanca stadium, Pope John Paul II did not hesitate to tell them: 'We believe in the same God, the one God, the living God, the God who creates the worlds and brings the worlds to their perfection.'[1] This is an indubitable affirmation of the *existence* of one and the same creator God. But one also has to add that Christians and Muslims who worship the same God have very different conceptions of God's unity. One could even say that the monotheism which is a common heritage of all the children of Abraham has at the same time divided them for centuries. Muslims cannot accept Christian monotheism as trinitarian monotheism, and that is a direct consequence of their rejection of the divine sonship of Jesus. That is why the indirect formulation of Vatican II in *Nostra aetate* 3 is certainly more prudent: 'The Church has also a high regard for the Muslims. They worship God, who is one, living and subsistent, merciful and almighty.'

So we should remember how by its radical nature, Islamic monotheism differs from Christian monotheism, and note that in Muslim eyes the sin *par excellence*, that of idolatry, is committed not only by pagan polytheists but also by Christians themselves. But at the same time, over and above engaging in a secular polemic, we may ask whether in the age of interfaith dialogue this difference should not lead both sides to vie with each other in seeking a God who is always greater.

## I. The dogma of the divine unity

Five times a day the ritual call to prayer, the famous *shahada*, resounds from the top of every minaret: 'There is no god but God, and Muhammad is his prophet.' This two-fold profession of faith sums up the whole faith of Islam. This affirmation of the absolute unity of God is based on the Qur'an, the last word of God revealed to human beings through Muhammad, the last of the prophets. This revelation is not new: it seeks to confirm and restore in its initial purity the radical monotheism to which the whole biblical tradition bears witness, but which was altered first by the Jews and then by the Christians. Thus the last of the prophets is in a line of prophets which goes back to Adam; among them the most famous figures were Noah, Abraham, Moses and Jesus. So it can be said that the Muslim creed goes back to the *shema Israel*. The prophetic vocation of Islam is to claim the absolute rights of the one God in the face of any form of idolatry as this was to be found at its beginnings, in the polytheism of the pagan Bedouins of Mecca or later among the Judaized Arabs and even the Christians at Medina.[2]

However, even when we consider the first preaching of the Prophet, it would be wrong to claim that Islamic monotheism is an extension of Jewish monotheism. The two forms of monotheism are in fact profoundly different. The monotheism of Israel which emerged progressively is above all soteriological ('There is no other God than Yahweh who is a saviour,' Hos. 13.4; Isa. 45.21) and it is inseparable from the unique covenant made with the chosen people. It could be said that Islamic monotheism is essentially ontological and dogmatic and has no link with a historical covenant.[3] If we are intent on speaking of covenant, it denotes uniquely the initial covenant (*mîthâq*) of Adam with his creator. The oneness of God is inscribed on human nature as it was originally; it is the famous *fitrah* or prime nature of human beings. According to a *hadith*, the Prophet says: 'Every new-born is born Muslim; it is his parents who make him Jew, Christian or Mazdaean.' Thus, while the biblical revelation is inseparable from a history of salvation marked by successive covenants which find their fulfilment in the new covenant in Christ, the new Qur'anic revelation has no connection with a sacred history of which God is the agent. Strictly speaking, there is no 'progress in revelation', since all the prophets prior to Muhammad hand on the same message about divine unity and we can note a kind of 'dehistoricization' of sacred history as it is related in the Bible.[4]

The name of Allah, which is a contraction of 'Al-Illah, is not a creation of Muhammad's and was already in use in pre-Islamic Arabia. It does not so much denote a particular God as the deity in general incarnated in a multitude of local gods. The prime mission of the Prophet is to announce that from now on Allah sums up all divinity to the exclusion of other gods. Surah 112, called *Tahwid* (i.e. the uniqueness of God), is one of the most famous surahs of the Qur'an and can often be found engraved on mosques and in houses: 'Say, He is God, the Only One (*samad*),[5] God, the Everlasting

Refuge who has not begotten, and has not been begotten, and equal to Him is not any one.' One could rightly say that the revelation of the Qur'an relates less to the existence of God than to his uniqueness. That is why the most serious sin, for which there is no forgiveness, is *shirk*, i.e. *associating* other gods with God.

## II. The sin *par excellence*

When the prophet thinks of those who associate other gods with God he has in view primarily the polytheists of Mecca who regarded the three goddesses honoured in their temple as 'daughters of Allah' (cf. surah 37.149–153). But above all during the Medina period he also has in view Jews who have succumbed to idolatry and Christians who claim to make Jesus the son of God (cf. surahs 4.17; 9.30 and 31; 19.34 and 35). It is in the Medina surahs that the full name of Jesus appears: 'The Christ Jesus son of Mary.' But the Qur'an specifies in surah 9.30 that 'The Christian says, "The Messiah is the Son of God."' That is the sin *par excellence*, the sin of associationism which vitiates the uniqueness and the transcendence of God; moreover it is absurd, for how could God most High or any Other incarnate Himself in a human body?

Thus Islam firmly refuses to recognize the divine Sonship of Jesus, the son of Mary, even if it considers him to be a unique prophet to the degree that he is not included – as Muhammad is – in the sequence of human generations. He is the Word (*kalima*) who emanates from God: 'We breathed into her of Our Spirit (surah 21.19; 66.12). And Ibn Arabi does not hesitate to designate Jesus 'the seal of holiness', while Muhammad is proclaimed 'the seal of the prophets' (surah 33.40). We also know the attachment of Muslims to the virgin birth of Jesus. But Christians conclude wrongly from this that he is a child of God. How could God have a child? 'Allah is only One God. Glory be to Him – that he should have a son! To Him belongs all that is in the heavens and in the earth; God suffices for a guardian' (surah 4.171). Breaking with paganism, like Jews and Christians, Muslims reject any carnal generation on the part of God (the name 'Father' is not one of the ninety-nine divine names). But they always take the name Father in a literal sense and seem incapable of understanding what a spiritual and eternal generation in the Christian sense could be. So their rejection of the dogma of the incarnation is inseparable from their rejection of the trinitarian monotheism of Christians.

It is because they are thought to have introduced associationism into God

himself that the Christians are accused, following the Jews, of having falsified the scriptures: 'They are unbelievers who say "God is the Third of
Three." No God is there but One God' (surah 5.78). One could think that
the criticism of a trinitarian conception of God is aimed only at a caricature
of the God confessed by the Christian faith. And in fact, curiously enough
we find in the Qur'an the idea of an insertion of Mary into the very heart of
the trinitarian God by virtue of a certain identification with the Spirit.[6] That
is the case in surah 5.116: 'O Jesus, son of Mary, didst thou say unto men,
"Take me and my mother as gods, apart from God?"' But it would be illusory to think that Islam rejects only a caricature of the Christian doctrine of
the Trinity. As later Muslim theology shows in its polemic against the Arab
Christian theologians who sought to spell out the notions of 'person' and
'nature' in Arabic, Islam radically challenges even an orthodox conception of
the dogma of the Trinity. This trinity of persons is in fact contrary to the
absolute oneness of God not only externally (no other God) but internally,
where God is indivisible, indissociable (which is one of the meanings of the
word *samad* that we have already met).

This univocal conception of the internal unity of God is all the stranger
since Muslim theologians, like mediaeval Jewish and Christian theologians,
used every subtlety to reconcile the diversity of the divine names with the
divine simplicity. But they in particular understood perfectly that the names
of Father, Son and Spirit are different from the divine attributes: they
denote persons in God. Whatever may be the Arabic translation of the
notion of person, in their view it could only end up in tritheism.

## III. The prophecy of Islam as a warning

The denial of the fundamental dogmas of Christianity, the incarnation and
the Trinity, makes Muslim-Christian dialogue particularly difficult. However, this dialogue always remains open, for we have not yet reached the
end of the historical reasons for such a misunderstanding between the two
monotheisms. If we remember that in the Qur'an the specific function of
Muhammad, as of the former prophets, is not to give a prediction about the
future but to issue both a reminder and a warning (a reminder of the identical Word of God and a warning of the new signs of God's rights), we may
think that Islam as a revelation and a practical attitude serves as a warning
about the inadequate conceptions and practices of Christians where
monotheism is concerned.

Christian trinitarian monotheism seeks to be no less intransigent than that of Islam. But it has to be noted that Christian theology has never ceased to attempt to reconcile the uniqueness of God with the trinity of persons. And over the centuries theologians have always had difficulty in guarding against the two symmetrical dangers of modalism[7] and tritheism. Great theologians like Karl Barth and Karl Rahner, aware of the ambiguity of the notion of person, which today no longer denotes a metaphysical auxiliary (hypostasis) but primarily a centre of conscience, seek to do away with the idea of a vulgar tritheism. Thus Rahner tries to understand the divine persons as distinct modes of divine subsistence. However, for Moltmann this idealistic modalism reduces the doctrine of the Trinity to a monotheism of a single essence, a single conscience and a single freedom. Ultimately what we have is the same identical subject in triplicate. Contrary to the Western tradition, which since Augustine has started from the unity of the divine essence, in conformity to the witness of scripture it is important to begin from the three persons who manifest themselves in the history of Christ. So Moltmann wants to substitute the trinitarian concept of unitedness for the philosophical concept of unity: 'For only the concept of unitedness is the concept of a unity that can be communicated and is open. The one God is a God *at one* with himself.'[8] He even goes so far as to proscribe the term monotheism for designating the mystery of the Trinity. Such a demand is not only contrary to the whole of Christian tradition but makes even more difficult the dialogue with Islam, which will always suspect a new form of tritheism. It would be wiser to remember, following Thomas Aquinas, that the trinity of persons does not divide the unity of divine essence, since the persons are distinct only according to their original relations. Thus in the uni-trinity of God no person is another, but each person is God. There are not three gods, and there are not three modes of being of a single subjectivity either.

The break with Islam relates both to the mystery of the Trinity and the mystery of the incarnation. But here again the intransigent monotheism of Islam can today be a salutary warning to Christians when they seek to confess the divinity of Jesus without attacking the absolute rights of God. Jesus is God, but *qua* Son of God, and we know that the non-biblical term 'incarnation' is no more than a metaphor. The mystery of the incarnation remains intact beyond the expressions which seek to take account of it. According to the earliest witnesses of the Christian tradition, the divine sonship does not relate primarily to the mystery of the incarnation but to Easter, to the mystery of Christ's exaltation and resurrection. The first Christians confessed Jesus as Christ, i.e. as the one 'in whom the whole fullness of the deity dwells bodily' (Col.2.9). But that does not absolutize the humanity of Jesus. For Christians, as for Muslims, only the God of Jesus, the creator of all humankind, is absolutely unique. Jesus is not an emanation of God. That is why certain theologians today prefer to speak of the identity of Jesus in terms of enthronement rather than of eternal generation.[9] The divine sonship is not of the order of a physical or even a metaphysical generation – which Islam cannot accept – but is an enthronement by God. This would avoid what looks like bitheism.

Some historians think that the prophet Muhammad could have known Christians influenced by Ebonite currents who recognized the virgin birth of Jesus but rejected his pre-existence.[10] Hence his violent objections to the divine sonship of Jesus, which he always understands in a carnal sense. The Christian faith which found its expression at Nicaea (325) and Chalcedon (451) would deny itself if it no longer confessed the divine identity of Jesus. But it would doubtless be possible in future to pursue a fruitful dialogue with Islam, starting from a narrative christology of Jesus as servant of God. The Acts of the Apostles in particular bears witness to this, and it is very different from the descending christology which then developed in the Hellenistic world under the influence of St Paul.

## IV. A God ever greater

I have suggested that we can discern in Islam a warning in the sense of a call to the quest of a God who is every greater. Christians can in turn take up the invocation proclaimed by every muezzin several times a day: Allahu Akbar (God is great! God alone is great).[11] How can we fail to recognize that some Christian formulations about the Trinity are often verbal, or at least inadequate, because they risk compromising the uniqueness of God and ending up in a form of tritheism? And likewise, there is a way of understanding the divinity of Jesus which can damage the absolute transcendence of God and lead to a form of bitheism.

However, in the age of interfaith dialogue, has not the time come to go beyond a polemic which gets nowhere and to see how the difference between the monotheism of Islam and Christian monotheism can help both sides to get a better grasp of the meaning of the true transcendence of God? We have a shared responsibility to confess a personal God in the face of modern unbelief and the increasing attraction of transcendences without God. Christians with a trinitarian faith must allow themselves to be asked questions by Muslims, to the degree that Islam demands strict monotheism no less firmly. But conversely, how could the doctors of Islam who proclaim the uniqueness and greatness of God so passionately ignore the revelation of the Fatherhood of God in Jesus Christ?[12]

Rather than persevere in a banal and ultimately incorrect contrast between the distant God of Islam and the near God of Christianity, we should take account of the tension between two radically different conceptions of the divine oneness and investigate their historical and philosophical roots. Even if the Qur'anic revelation seeks only to be the confirmation of the biblical revelation of the exclusive unity of the creator God, we can seriously ask whether the transcendence of the God of Islam does not finally obey the philosophical logic of the Absolute, i.e. that of the identity which excludes all difference and is the expression of its self-sufficiency. That seems difficult to contest when we come to later Muslim theology, which has the marks of its encounter with the capital of Greek thought. But more radically, must we not follow Louis Massignon in discerning in the Qur'anic revelation a natural theology which differs from the salvation-historical theology developed by the sacred writers of Israel?

On the other hand, if we follow Christian monotheism through to the end as an affirmation of the uni-trinity of God, we discover that the uniqueness of God must be thought of as a unity which assumes differences. The God of trinitarian monotheism is a life differentiated in communion. It is there that the originality of the God of Christians proves to be so different from the God of natural theology. And because God is in himself a mystery of communication, he tends to communicate to the maximum in human history. The supreme expression of this communication is the mystery of the incarnation, i.e. the covenant of the eternal and almighty God with the ephemera of history,

Now far from attacking the absolute transcendence of God – as Islam always claims – this *future* of God points us, rather, to a more demanding conception of God's transcendence, a transcendence in love and not according to the logic of the identity of the absolute Being with itself. The mystery consists in the very fact that the pathos of God does not compromise his transcendent Otherness. Because the transcendence of God is a transcendence in love and not simply one of being, it can take the paradoxical form of a certain humility, of kenosis or even – to use Hans Jonas' terms – of a certain impotence.

In conclusion, the confrontation of the two monotheisms has not ended up being a stimulus for all the sons of Abraham. The God who reveals himself as Father, Son and Spirit raises questions for the God of Islam who is ever greater, above all when Muslim thought has to confront the excess of evil in history. But at the same time, the strange prophecy of the Qur'an which arose seven centuries after the coming of Christ can be accepted as a warning by Christians, seeing that it bears witness to the same unique God who is revealed to Abraham, Moses and Jesus. Here we need not undertake a Christian reading of the Qur'an. Rather, we must welcome it in its very difference as a witness to an original experience of God in which certain authentic aspects of the greatness of God are not expressed as they are in the teaching and practice of Christianity.

*Translated by John Bowden*

### Notes

1. *Documentation catholique*, 6 October 1985, no. 1903, 942.
2. We know that the composition of the Qur'an as it now exists does not follow the chronology of the life of the Prophet and the recitation of the Qur'an. The shortest surahs, which correspond to the Mecca period, are put at the end, and the longest, which were recited at Medina, are put at the beginning. It is these latest surahs which are most violent about Jews and Christians. 'Whereas in the first Mecca period the recitation of the Qur'an came close to the biblical tradition, with Moses as the main figure, the late surahs of the Qur'an (3, 4, 5) attack Judaism violently and distance themselves from the Christian presentation of Jesus Christ, to such a degree that at this moment the Qur'an no longer included Judaism and Christianity in the authentic monotheism of Islam, as was the case in the early period at Mecca.' Cf. E. Platti, *Islam . . . étrange?*, Paris 2000, p.152.
3. See especially R. Caspar, 'The Permanent Significance of Israel's Monotheism', *Concilium* 177, 1985, pp.67–78.
4. 'For the Qur'an, revelation takes place only by the transmission of a unique Word of God which is always identical to itself; it does not take its place in a history which evolves by adapting to it. It reveals what has always been and always will be if God wills it'; Platti, op.cit., p.91.
5. There has been a discussion of how to translate *samad*: 'in fullness', 'indissociable', 'impenetrable', 'the only One'. For this see J. Jomier, *Dieu et l'homme dans le Coran*, Paris 1996, pp.188–89.
6. Several authors have noted this representation of the Spirit as mother in some of the apocrypha and some church fathers; see Platti, op.cit., p.175.
7. This is the name given to the heresy according to which the Father, the Son and the Spirit are only manifestations or different modes of a single divine person. Constantly the term tritheism is used when the Trinity is conceived of in such a way that the absolute unity of the divine essence breaks up into three Gods. A

contemporary theologian like Jürgen Moltmann has accused Karl Barth and Karl Rahner of finally ending up in a kind of modalism on the pretext of avoiding tritheism.

8. J. Moltmann, *The Trinity and the Kingdom of God*, London and New York 1981, p.150.

9. Here I am particularly thinking of the most original work by Joseph Moingt, *L'homme qui venait de Dieu*, Paris 1993.

10. The name Ebionite is used to denote a number of Jewish-Christian groups attached to the Jerusalem community who regarded Jesus as an ordinary man. They lived according to the Jewish law and rejected the teaching of St Paul.

11. Cf. Jomier, op.cit., especially Chapter X, 'La grandeur de Dieu', which is very fine.

12. I have already mentioned this reciprocal emulation of Christianity and Islam in my article 'La portée théologique du dialogue islamo-chrétien', *Islamochristiana* 18, 1999, pp.1–23. Recently I have put the same question again in another study, 'Le pluralisme religieux de l'indifférentisme ou le vrai défi de la théologie chrétienne', *Revue théologique de Louvain* 31, 2000, pp.3–32.

# A New Daring of the Religious Imagination: 'God' in Feminist Theology

ELAINE WAINWRIGHT

The imagination is accessible not primarily to abstract ideas but to language, images, interpersonal experience, symbolism, art – all the integrated approaches which appeal simultaneously to intellect, will, and feeling. What must be undertaken is a therapy of the religious imagination, first in regard to God and then in regard to our relationship with Jesus Christ.[1]

Religious language begins in lively metaphor, babbling a vision, exploding with ecstasy, nurturing human community.[2]

This contribution undertakes *a* reading of the 'therapy of the religious imagination' in regard to 'God'[3] that has been characteristic of the current feminist movement's last two decades or more of feminist theologizing. Faithful to a key characteristic of feminist theology, it begins with women's *experience* of the naming of 'God', an experience both given to them and taken from them.[4] The focus then shifts to women's *speaking* 'God' in a new and daring voice in the story, imagery and metaphors of the Christian tradition as these have been reclaimed in dialogue with biblical, theological and women's wisdom traditions. Women's *addressing* 'God' in liturgy, ritual and community prayer and *encountering* 'God' in religious experience and spirituality likewise constitute key aspects of such a reading as these elements have been integrally interwoven in feminist theology's engagement with divinity. While the vision/ecstasy/mystery may need to be separated from experience or 'nurturing human community' for the purpose of reading, it is evident among many feminist theologians that such a distinction is not faithful to either the experienced mystery or the ethical experience of Christian feminism and its goal of human transformation.[5]

Before this reading begins, it is important to clarify the term 'feminist theology'. Some may understand it as a single unitary sub-set of 'theology', undertaken prospectively and hence considered inferior to the 'theology' of those who do not name their perspective. Indeed, it is undertaken prospectively, grounded in the experience of women who constitute half of humanity and whose voices are raised from a multiplicity of subject positions shaped not only by gender but by race, ethnicity, class, religious history. Feminist theology is not, however, single or unitary. Rather, it is a creative multi-voiced process of theologizing which dialogues with a variety of sources both past and present in order to speak 'God' anew in a myriad of ways into the lives of a multi-faceted Christianity facing into a new millennium. The reading to follow will seek to allow some of these many voices to be heard.

## I. Articulating the experience

Many shifts in consciousness among women accompanied the women's/feminist movement of the latter half of the twentieth century. These brought to awareness the naming of 'God' in male-only language and imagery within the Christian theological tradition and worship; the structures of injustice within churches based on gender;[6] the intimate relationship between these two issues; and their impact on women's religious lives and imagination. As Sallie McFague noted as early as 1982, 'it is not just that "God the father" is a frequent appellation for the divine, but that the entire structure of divine-human and human-human relationships is understood in a patriarchal framework'.[7] She goes on to indicate that 'religious language is not only religious but also human, not only about God but also about us'.[8] Schneiders articulates at least one overarching outcome of the interconnectedness of male-dominated language and structures: 'it has a destructive effect on women's spiritual self-image and perverts their relationships with male Christians and with God'.[9] For María Clara Bingemer, 'the patriarchal God that marks Judaism and Christianity' is closely linked to men's position of power in society'.[10]

Analysis of the profound interrelationship between the naming of 'God' and women's experiences of exclusionary church structures and practices focussed the attention of many feminist theologians on the nature of religious language. Sallie McFague examined this issue extensively in *Metaphorical Theology*, pointing out that 'either to equate human words with the divine reality or to see no relationship between them is inappropriate'.[11] Rather, she suggested that a 'metaphorical' approach was needed, one characterized by Phyllis Trible's image – 'like a finger pointing to the moon'.[12] Elizabeth Johnson's critique of 'traditional speech about God' as 'humanly oppressive and religiously idolatrous',[13] lead her to develop an approach which holds in tension the mystery of 'God' and the affirmation of human and cosmic liberation:

> . . . only if the full reality of women as well as men enters into the symbol-ization of God along with symbols from the natural world, can idolatrous fixation on one image be broken and the truth of the mystery of God, in tandem with the liberation of all human beings and the whole earth, emerge for our time.[14]

Both experientially and analytically, feminist theologians have named their experience. From a theoretical perspective, Serene Jones has examined that naming and has placed its varied modes along a spectrum between 'methodologically essentialized' and 'radically historicized'.[15] She invites feminist theologians to continue the conversation around experience so that they hold in tension results that offer 'enduring wisdoms and sturdy graces' and those 'rupturing voices and more particularized graces'[16] that suspend the question of truth and stability. The new daring of the religious imagina-tion within feminist theology has not yet finished. It has barely begun as women's articulation, analysis and critique continue to uncover the depths of the problems and the pain which lie at the heart of the Christian tradition which is founded on a gospel of incarnation in all flesh and liberation for all – human and other than human – but which maintains both a theology and a structure centred on maleness alone. If the gospel is to speak into the twenty-first millennium, the analyses of feminist theology must be taken seriously by all responsible Christian theologians and the question of experience as a source for Christian theologizing explored across all theolo-gies.

## II. Speaking 'God' in story, imagery and metaphor

With increasing hermeneutical sophistication, feminist biblical scholars and feminist theologians have brought their analyses of women's experience into dialogue with the received tradition in a way that has placed them in line with the prophets of that tradition. Walter Brueggemann characterizes the prophetic role as two-fold: criticizing and energizing.[17] The general feminist hermeneutic of deconstruction and reconstruction[18] mirrors the two-fold prophetic task as categorized by Brueggemann. It has been given first a four-fold and then seven-fold expression by Elisabeth Schüssler Fiorenza. In *Bread not Stone*, her feminist biblical hermeneutic moves interactively between suspicion or critique, remembrance and reconstruction, proclamation, and creative actualization. In this way, she links the work of biblical interpretation to the liturgical and spiritual/experiential lives of women within the *ekklesia gynaikon*.[19] Later she develops her basic framework, adding a hermeneutics of experience and social location, an analytic of domination, and a hermeneutics of transformation.[20] She also explores the ethical/rhetorical function of feminist liberation theologies in terms of the worlds they create for all women, especially the poorest and most marginalized.

In speaking anew the 'God' of the biblical tradition, Schüssler Fiorenza has augmented Trible's uncovering of the *rachamim*/'womb compassion' and the Eros of God.[21] She brings to light that religious imagination of the past which named the 'female Gestalt' of 'God' as Sophia and as the Sophia 'God' of Jesus across the biblical testaments of wisdom writers and evangelists.[22] Reclamation of the traditions of Sophia have profoundly enriched women's *speaking* 'God' in Christianity's retraditioning process[23] because she is both transcendent and immanent. She was with the Creative One at the foundation of the universe (Prov. 8.22–30) but she likewise delights in the human community (Prov. 8.31), pitching her tent in their midst (Ecclus. 24.8–12) and inviting them to both love and to live righteousness (Wisd. 1.1) as the wisdom tradition testifies. This biblical tradition of Sophia has been augmented as scholars have explored its roots in earlier female images of divinity; its later manifestation within Judaism,[24] Christianity,[25] and other wisdom traditions;[26] and her impact in women's lives. The language and imagery of Sophia has enabled women to speak 'God' in a way that has enlivened their spirit, sharpened their 'vision' and given a new voice to their 'ecstasy'. Within this reclamation, however, there is a need to remember that many of the traditions of Sophia were shaped within androcentric scribal schools and philosophical traditions and that this aspect needs a thorough and ongoing critique.[27]

Maternal images of 'God' – birthing, feeding, nurturing, compassionate, guiding, and fiercely protective, the she-bear, the mother eagle, the mother – burst forth from the religious imagination captured in both the biblical and theological/spiritual traditions.[28] They are providing a rich source for the spirituality, for the new religious imagination of women and men today as they did for their ancestors. There is a danger, however, that too great or too

solitary an emphasis on maternal images for divinity will function mono-
lithically to affirm a biological role for women within the churches while
they remain profoundly patriarchal. Tikva Frymer-Kensky captures the
paradoxical nature of such imaging.

> When modeling is done by the divine, the modeling does not simply
> illustrate; it authorizes and approves what it models. This is a powerful
> two-edged sword. On the one hand, divine modeling for women's family
> roles gives women esteem within these roles . . . On the other hand, this
> same divine modeling makes cultural attitudes and stereotypes part of the
> realm of the sacred, lending powerful support to these attitudes and
> inhibiting change.[29]

Feminist theologizing in relation to divinity must not become fixed,
static or singular but must remain actively engaged in ongoing critique/
reclamation even in relation to its own articulations and effects.

A profound problem faced within feminist theology's 'therapy of the
religious imagination' is the naming of the Trinity in anthropocentric terms,
especially Father and Son. Both Catherine LaCugna and Elizabeth A.
Johnson have addressed what they see as the defeat or the demise of trinitarian faith within Christianity not only because of its exclusive male
imagery but also its loss of connectedness to the gospel message of liberation.
For LaCugna, the reclamation of Trinity lies in the Cappadocian relational
trinity best expressed in the model of *perichoresis*, 'being-in-one-another,
permeation without confusion',[30] a dance of interrelationship. But such a
theology and doxology, she claims, must be lived in the continuation of the
reign-of-God which characterized the life and work of Jesus and which is
storied in the Christian gospels.[31] Johnson too reclaims the *perichoresis* of
the Trinity in dialogue with the biblical tradition or narrative, naming the
movement between Spirit-Sophia, Jesus-Sophia and Mother-Sophia in the
terminology of biblical wisdom.[32]

The religious imagination of many women and some men is being shaped
anew from the wealth of received tradition reclaimed within a feminist perspective. Tragically, however, for the churches, this is being virtually
ignored within mainstream Christian theology. Lest I be considered a biased
observer, let me quote Erhard S. Gerstenberger:

> Discussions by contemporary male systematic theologians (still?) seem
> not to take the feminist critique of God with great seriousness . . . [I]t

seems to me that a critical and open male contribution to the present theological discussion of feminist challenges to our imaging of God is dangerously underrepresented. Theological truth can only be approached by the open conversation of everyone involved.[33]

And this conversation is not just essential but urgent. It must be an engagement of the hermeneutical, methodological and prophetic aspects of feminist theology and not just a dismissal from a priestly and foundationalist position. The urgency is not because 'God' is under threat. Rather, the human community, the reign-of-God community is seriously under threat since it is nurtured by its imaging of 'God' for its work of liberation.

## III. Addressing 'God' in liturgy, ritual and community prayer

The traditional context in which the Christian community's belief and its communal voice raised in prayer intersect is the liturgy (*lex orandi lex credendi*). While the language of liturgical prayer has been addressed by many feminist theologians as one implication of their speaking 'God' anew in story imagery and metaphors, it is liturgists such as Gail Ramshaw and Marjorie Procter-Smith who have highlighted the radical and daring implications of this new speech in the context of communal prayer.[34] As a conclusion to her own explorations of new ways of speaking the biblical and trinitarian 'God', Ramshaw looks to what she calls 'continual and faithful reformation'. Sensitive to the worship context as not primarily a 'vehicle for consciousness-raising', she nevertheless places radical challenges before the churches, concluding that 'were the search for more faithful speech to mark the church, the speech itself would not be far behind . . . We can concede that this will be a hundred-year project, but only if the church is zealously engaged in the endless and exacting tasks of reform today.'[35] What a daring challenge to churches encompassing many cultures, theologies and experiences.[36]

And since most women know that the project of both speaking and addressing 'God' anew will be both long and characterized by painful struggle and ongoing exclusion from the language of formal liturgies, they have developed rituals to celebrate their religious lives; to nurture their religious imaginations; and to sustain their spiritual journeys. It is in these contexts that Asian and African women can name 'God' in the images, language and symbols of their ancient cultures and contemporary life experiences;[37] and African-American women can tell the stories of their foremothers and their knowing of 'God'.[38] Here too indigenous women, women of colour from many different cultures can dance, can sing, can address their 'God' in ways that spring forth from the depths of their being and their ancient cultures. The religious imagination of countless women from countless contexts across human history is the source of women's new ritual expression and experience.

## IV. Encountering 'God' in religious experience and spirituality

We have come full-circle it would seem and yet we are but at the beginning. For many women, the new naming of 'God' is born out of experience informed by wisdom. This is nowhere more obvious than in the stories told by Ada Maria Isasi-Diaz and Yolanda Tarango in *Hispanic Women: Prophetic Voice in the Church*.[39] Such stories are being told in women's gatherings, both formal and informal, across the globe. Women are undertaking a daring new project, they are shaping a new religious imagination that is enabling them to speak, to address and to encounter 'God' in ways that are life-enriching for their own spirits and for their engagement in the gospel project of liberation, the enacting of the reign-of-God. This new imagination is finding creative articulation in the visual arts, music, dance and ritual.

There is so much more that could be said to explore the threads that connect feminist theology with other liberation theologies, with ecological theologizing,[40] with post-colonial perspectives; to highlight the significance of embodiment in contemporary feminist spirituality; to trace the thealogical traditions. This, however, is not *the* definitive reading but *a* reading of feminist theologies' speaking, addressing, and encountering the divine. It has emerged that these are multi-vocal, bubbling forth images, metaphors and stories that are both ancient and new, multi-cultural and multi-focal. They have emerged from women being graced with a recognition of their need to nurture a new religious imagination if they are to sustain a life-enhancing relationship with their own selves, with others in the human and earth communities and with the 'God' whom they have encountered as mystery. The churches are being offered this same grace. Throughout this article, I have sought to articulate some of the challenges which accompany this grace. For the sake of the future not only of the human but the entire planetary community, we can but hope that a new daring may characterize all those in the churches who speak, address and encounter the one they call 'God'.

## Notes

1. Sandra M. Schneiders, *Women and the Word*, 1986 Madeleva Lecture in Spirituality, New York: Paulist Press 1986, p.19.

2. Gail Ramshaw, *God beyond Gender: Feminist Christian God-Language*, Minneapolis: Fortress Press 1985, p.6.

3. It needs to be acknowledged at the outset that the very designation 'God' is problematic within feminist theology. This has been highlighted most particularly by Elisabeth Schüssler Fiorenza who uses the designation G*d in order to draw attention to the patriarchal imagination which has shaped the connotations which the word 'God' evokes for both women and men. See Elisabeth Schüssler Fiorenza, *Jesus: Miriam's Child, Sophia's Prophet*, New York: Continuum and London: SCM Press 1995, p.191. See also Fran Gray, 'G*d's Excludedness: Beyond Language, Beyond the World: a Levinasian Reading of *Ekklesia Gynaikon*', *Australian Feminist Studies* 14.30 (1999), pp.333–44.

4. Mary Daly, *Beyond God the Father: Toward a Philosophy of Women's Liberation*, Boston: Beacon Press 1973, p.8, claims that 'women have had the power of naming stolen from us', while so much of women's articulation of their experience demonstrates the givenness of the naming of 'God' within religious contexts whose theology and structures have been dominated by androcentrism and male control throughout history.

5. Sandra M. Schneiders, *Beyond Patching: Faith and Feminism in the Catholic Church*, The Anthony Jordan Lectures, Newman Theological College, New York: Paulist Press 1991, p.36, says of this transformation that it 'will be in the direction of salvation for the race and for the planet' or in the stream of the gospel tradition it could be named as the kin-dom preached by Jesus, God's transformative dream with and for humanity and the earth community.

6. Feminist theology has been undertaken across a wide variety of Christian denominations and beyond the churches with only limited need to distinguish the injustices particular to one denomination rather than another.

7. Sallie McFague, *Metaphorical Theology: Models of God in Religious Language*, Philadelphia: Fortress Press and London: SCM Press 1982, p.8.

8. McFague, *Metaphorical Theology*, p.10.

9. Schneiders, *Women and the Word*, p.5.

10. María Clara Bingemer, 'Reflections on The Trinity' in Elsa Tamez (ed), *Through Her Eyes: Women's Theology from Latin America*, Maryknoll: Orbis 1989, p.60. It should be noted here that women's experience of the effect of the naming of 'God' has been articulated from many different perspectives – womanist, *mujerista*, Hispanic, Asian, African, women of colour and white Western, and from multiple subject positions within those categories including post-Christian. Feminist theology seeks to listen to and give expression to these myriad voices. See by way of example, Ursula King (ed), *Feminist Theology from*

the Third World: A Reader,* Maryknoll: Orbis 1994. Unfortunately, in a short essay, all cannot be heard simultaneously.

11. McFague, *Metaphorical Theology*, p.7.

12. Phyllis Trible, *God and the Rhetoric of Sexuality*, Overtures to Biblical Theology, Philadelphia: Fortress Press 1978, p.16.

13. Elizabeth A. Johnson, *She Who Is: The Mystery of God in Feminist Theological Discourse*, New York: Crossroad 1992, p.18.

14. Johnson, *She Who Is*, p.56.

15. Serene Jones, 'Women's Experience between a Rock and a Hard Place: Feminist, Womanist, and *Mujerista* Theologies in North America' in Rebecca S. Chopp and Sheila Greeve Davaney (eds), *Horizons in Feminist Theology: Identity, Tradition and Norms*, Minneapolis: Fortress Press 1997, p.33.

16. Jones, 'Women's Experience', p.53.

17. Walter Brueggemann, *The Prophetic Imagination*, Philadelphia: Fortress Press 1978, pp.44–79.

18. Seyla Benhabib and Drucilla Cornell, 'Introduction: Beyond the Politics of Gender' in Seyla Benhabib and Drucilla Cornell (eds), *Feminism as Critique*, Minneapolis: University of Minnesota Press 1987, p.1.

19. Elisabeth Schüssler Fiorenza, *Bread not Stone: The Challenge of Feminist Biblical Interpretation*, Tenth Anniversary Edition, Boston: Beacon Press 1995, pp.1–22.

20. Elisabeth Schüssler Fiorenza, *Rhetoric and Ethic: The Politics of Biblical Studies*, Minneapolis: Fortress Press 1999, pp.48–55.

21. Trible, *God and the Rhetoric of Sexuality*, pp.31–71, 72–165.

22. Elisabeth Schüssler Fiorenza, *In Memory of Her: A Feminist Theological Reconstruction of Christian Origins*, New York: Crossroad and London: SCM Press 1983, pp.130–40; *Sharing Her Word: Feminist Biblical Interpretation in Context*, Boston: Beacon Press 1998; and *Jesus: Miriam's Child*, pp.131–62.

23. Within the Catholic tradition, the necessity of ongoing interpretation and re-articulation was expressed succinctly by Cardinal Joseph Ratzinger in his introduction to the 1993 Pontifical Biblical Commission's document 'The Interpretation of the Bible in the Church', *Origins* 23.29 (1994), p.498: 'The study of the Bible . . . is never finished; each age must in its own way newly seek to understand the sacred books.'

24. Lynn Gottlieb, *She Who Dwells Within: A Feminist Vision of a Renewed Judaism*, New York: Harper San Francisco 1995, pp.13–48, explores traditions of *Shekinah*, the Dwelling or Abiding One imaged female in the kabbalist tradition. She traces her origins, however, not to the Wisdom tradition but to the Presence of 'God' in both the exodus and exilic traditions. See also Tikva Frymer-Kensky, *In the Wake of the Goddesses: Women, Culture, and the Biblical Transformation of Pagan Myth*, New York: Free Press 1992.

25. Josephine Griffiths, *The Reclaiming of Wisdom: The Restoration of the Feminine*

*in Christianity*, London: Avon Books 1994.

26. Caitlín Matthews, *Sophia - Goddess of Wisdom: The Divine Feminine from Black Goddess to World-Soul*, London: Mandala 1991.

27. Schüssler Fiorenza, *Jesus: Miriam's Child*, pp.155–62.

28. Virginia Ramey Mollenkott, *The Divine Feminine: The Biblical Imagery of God as Female*, New York: Crossroad 1983; Bridget Mary Meehan, *Exploring the Feminine Face of God*, Kansas City: Sheed & Ward 1991 and *Delighting in the Feminine Divine*, Kansas City: Sheed & Ward 1994; and Eleanor Rae and Bernice Marie-Daly, *Created in Her Image: Models of the Feminine Divine*, New York: Crossroad 1990.

29. Frymer-Kensky, *In the Wake of the Goddesses*, p.25. See also Johnson, *She Who Is*, pp.47–57, for a critique of stereotypical 'feminine' traits for 'God' but, on the other hand, the necessity of equivalent female and male images. Since 'God' has been imaged almost exclusively as 'father' then the 'mother' image, within a vast array of images old and new, is a necessary corrective.

30. Catherine Mowry LaCugna, *God for Us: The Trinity and Christian Life*, New York: Harper San Francisco 1991, pp. 280–88.

31. LaCugna, *God for Us*, pp.382–411.

32. Johnson, *She Who Is*, pp.124–223. See also Patricia Fox, *God as Communion: John Zizioulas, Elizabeth Johnson and the Retrieval of the Symbol of the Triune God*, Collegeville: Liturgical Press, forthcoming.

33. Erhard S. Gerstenberger, *Yahweh the Patriarch: Ancient Images of God and Feminist Theology*, Minneapolis: Fortress Press 1996, pp.xi, xv.

34. Ramshaw, *God beyond Gender* and Marjorie Procter-Smith, *Praying with Our Eyes Open: Engendering Feminist Liturgical Prayer*, Nashville: Abingdon 1995.

35. Ramshaw, *God beyond Gender*, pp.131–35.

36. Chung Hyun Kung, 'To be Human is to be Created in God's Image' in *Feminist Theology from the Third World*, p.252 says that 'it is natural for Asian women to think of the Godhead as male and female because there are many male gods and female goddesses in Asian religious cultures'.

37. Mercy Amba Oduyoye, 'Women and Ritual in Africa' in Mercy Amba Oduyoye and Musimbi R. A. Kanyoro (eds), *The Will to Arise: Women, Tradition, and the Church in Africa*, Maryknoll: Orbis 1992.

38. Delores Williams, *Sisters in the Wilderness: The Challenge of Womanist God-Talk*, Maryknoll: Orbis 1993.

39. Ada Maria Isasi-Diaz and Yolanda Tarango, *Hispanic Women: Prophetic Voice in the Church*, San Francisco: Harper & Row 1988.

40. See most recently Ivone Gebara, *Longing for Running Water: Ecofeminism and Liberation*, Minneapolis: Fortress Press 1999.

# III. Divine Revelation, Hermeneutics and Truth

# Interreligious Encounter and the Fragmentary Experience of God

CHRISTOPH SCHWÖBEL

## I. Changes in Western society

### 1. From secularization to religious pluralism

The last quarter of the last century has seen a remarkable change in the attitudes towards religion. Until the mid-1970s secularization was regarded by many inside and outside the church as the key-word for the interpretation of the religious situation of the times. It was assumed that spheres of life which had formerly been shaped by a religious framework would be freed from the tutelage of their religious interpretation. This process was understood by most as a unified, irreversible and global transition from religion to secularity, encompassing all dimensions of culture. To many of its interpreters this movement appeared like the fruition of the dynamics of autonomy that had begun in the Enlightenment. However different the responses to this situation were, from resistance to all secularizing tendencies to the attempt to understand this process itself theologically by trying to express the secular meaning of the gospel or by offering a non-religious interpretation of religious concepts, the underlying assumption was the same: religion is on the retreat and has to make way for the new dominance of the secular.

Since the mid-1970s the situation has changed considerably. The religious revolution in Iran demonstrated that secularization is by no means an irreversible process. Rather, it can be the breeding-ground of a new kind of religious radicalism reversing the direction of secularization by bringing everything under religious rule. This was not an isolated event, but proved to be a global phenomenon. In many cultures the revival of religious orientations has demonstrated the profound influence of religion on all political and social questions. The revival of religious interest comprises both religions with a long tradition and new forms of religiosity. The growth of post-secular religiosities in industrialized countries is often combined with aspirations to return to less alienated forms of living which supposedly can be found in traditional religions and traditional lifestyles. Contrary to the predictions of popular secularization theories the twenty-first century appears at its beginning not as the century which might bring the end of religion but as a century characterized by a powerful renaissance of religious interest. Secularization has remained an influence in the religious situation, but it is neither a uniform trend nor is it irreversible.

The renaissance of religion has been experienced in many societies as the rise of a new religious pluralism. Religion, diagnosed by many as moribund in the first half of the twentieth century, makes a lively return at the end of the century – but it comes back in plural forms. Religious pluralism signifies a situation in society where a plurality of fundamental religious and ideological orientations exists in a state of coexistence or competition. This competition is inevitable if these religious orientations are based on convictions claiming to shape the whole life of their adherents because they are believed to offer insights of universal truth. This pluralistic situation is not entirely new. The cultural context of the Graeco-Roman Empire in which Christianity began its historical career can be characterized as one of religious pluralism which became a situation of open conflict when the unifying social fabric of the civil religion of the imperial cult tore, not least through the influence of Christianity. In many ways the new religious pluralism appears like the return of the situation of the early church.

## 2. The de-canonization of the Enlightenment and the re-canonization of religious traditions

One could argue that there is a connection between the rise of religious pluralism as the most radical form of pluralism and the eclipse of what is called by its defenders and critics alike the 'Enlightenment Project'. It was one of the attempts of the Enlightenment to provide a common foundation of non-traditional and confessionally neutral principles for all knowledge-claims in confessionally diverse societies marked by the destructive consequences of the religious wars of the seventeenth century. Such a common foundation could include elements of natural religion, the religion that is, it was believed, common to all humans on the basis of their common nature, but it had to exclude those claims of the historical confessions, the 'religions' as they were called in the seventeenth century, which had proved to be at the roots of confessional dissent. The Enlightenment project could only succeed if the religions as they were practised in the context of religious communities were banished from the public square and relegated to the realm of private piety. Whatever stance we take in the debate about the interpretation of our cultural situation as one of post-modernity, late modernity or reflexive modernity, the very fact of this discussion indicates that the principles of the Enlightenment are no longer taken for granted as defining the common ground of our societies. This has enormous consequences for all standards based on the principles of the Enlightenment, including the modern justification of human rights, the foundation of all ethics on the principle of moral autonomy and formal procedures of testing their universality. The plausibility crisis of the 'Enlightenment project' also questions one of its most significant implications: the privatization of religion. Religion re-enters the public square, but not as a unified phenomenon, but in the plural, as a set of highly diverse basic orientations claiming to provide meaning and orientation in life. The public square no longer represents the common ground of the tacit convictions of society, it becomes a highly contested space for the influence of different basic orientations. The loss of the Enlightenment principles as the universal canon for regulating the common life of modern societies leads to a new social significance of the different canons of religious traditions, including that of Christianity. The de-canonization of the principles of the Enlightenment leads to the re-canonization of religious traditions.

## 3. Globalization and interreligious encounter

The situation of religious pluralism is not only a phenomenon that requires to be discussed in intellectual attempts to 'read' our cultural situation in global perspective. It is also an element of ordinary day-to-day experience. External factors like the migration movements of whole populations caused by political and cultural oppression, economic injustice and religiously motivated persecutions, together with internal factors like the loss of a common orientational framework have created a new situation of interreligious encounter in many contexts of life. The big cities all over the world present a rich ecology of religious communities, practices, beliefs and convictions as diverse and complex as a tropical rain forest. The 'global village' created by the electronic communication media has relativized the geographical distance of religious communities and their original home-lands. This is perhaps one of the most perplexing features of globalization: The unifying medium of world-wide electronic communication systems creates the forum for the global encounter of religious diversity. We can no longer distance ourselves from interreligious encounter: other religions come close in the encounter with our neighbour. They can no longer be treated as abstract systems of beliefs represented in foreign cultures and religious practices performed at a safe distance in far away lands. They have human faces, the faces of our neighbours.

It is one of the marks of globalization that the problems presented by religious diversity and conflict between the religions are at the same time large-scale global problems that affect the whole of humankind and problems of day-to-day living in our different local situation. In the 'global village' local problems become global problems and global problems become local problems. With the loss of influence of political mechanism and strategies for dealing with these problems based on the nation states, the religions which transcend the boundaries of national states acquire an increasing significance for the problems that occur on the global stage and for all attempts at dealing with them non-violently in a spirit of justice. Interreligious encounter is not a meeting of people with similar but different religious tastes which are safely restricted in the private sphere. Rather, it appears that its public significance can hardly be exaggerated in the situation of globalization.

## II. Religious pluralism and the new experience of God

### *1. Interreligious encounter and the perspective of faith*

Religious pluralism which characterizes the global situation and becomes concrete in interreligious encounter in our daily lives cannot be treated as a fact of our cultural situation which is an interesting topic for sociological research and cultural theory, but leaves the faith of Christians, the doctrine of the church and Christian theology untouched. It is precisely in the context of Christian faith's relationship to the triune God who is confessed by the church as the creator, reconciler and consummator of the world that interreligious encounter raises its most burning questions. Christians who have found the meaning and direction of theirs lives in faith in God would falsify their faith in God as the ground of all being, meaning and truth if they tried to deal with the challenge of other religions outside their faith. Faith in the triune God thus becomes the context in which the question of the other religions is raised and ways for responding to it must be explored. This seems at first sight a rather trivial insight. However, its impact becomes clear if we take its implications seriously. For Christians there is no other perspective from which they could try to make sense of other religions as they encounter them in their neighbours. There is no perspective 'above' the concrete religions, no stand-point abstracted from the living communities of faith from which this question could be approached. Radical religious pluralism demands a radical perspectivism. However, this perspectivism is by no means relativistic. The statement that all religions are in principle equally valid ways to salvation, equally valid paths to the Ultimate, the common view of those kinds of philosophical monism which have wrongly claimed the name 'pluralism', is the one statement that cannot be made in a situation of radical pluralism in which every statement is bound to the perspective from which it is made. Radical pluralism is non-relativistic because it does not permit abstraction from the perspective of a particular faith.

Once we understand that as Christians our view and practice of interreligious encounter is bound to the perspective of Christian faith, this has a number of liberating consequences for our understanding of our own and of other religions. Insisting on the particular character of Christian faith opens our view for the particularities of other religions. We are made aware that 'religion' is only alive in the religions and can only be understood from their particular self-interpretations. The religions in their concrete forms of presenting themselves become the focus of our attention in interreligious encounter. Even the term 'religion' has at best a heuristic character in encountering the specific forms of religious orientation in the particular religion. We must also recognize that the term 'faith' which summarizes the Christian relationship to God and the Christian orientation in the world cannot easily be transferred to other religions. Talking about 'other faiths' becomes ambivalent. On the one hand, it is an expression of the expectation to find in other religions a basic orientation which is just as fundamental for the way people structure their lives as their faith is for Christians; on the other hand we must expect that this basic orientation has a very different content and form than Christian faith which as a human act is shaped by the content it comprises. Recognizing that for Christians interreligious encounter is bound to the perspective of Christian faith makes the encounter with other religions an encounter of genuine otherness.

Equally serious as the danger of abstracting from the specific perspective of our faith by attempting to assume a standpoint above all perspectives is the danger of absolutizing our perspective of faith. According to the Christian understanding faith is a gift of God, it is constituted by God for us, not by us. Faith as unconditional trust in God depends at every moment on

God's self-disclosure to us. It is the relationship to God which God constitutes by creating certainty in our hearts about the truth of the Gospel of Christ through the Holy Spirit. The life of faith that is enabled by God's self-disclosure is a life lived in human responsibility to God, but it becomes never independent of God's action in creating faith. Faith never becomes a human possession, a religious property which is at our disposal. Because of its character as a dynamic relationship with the triune God Christian faith never remains dependent on God sustaining, nurturing and perfecting our faith. Christian faith is therefore never absolute. It is relative in so far as it is relational, in so far as it points away from itself to God as its ground and source, the only true Absolute. The Christian perspective of faith can therefore never claim to be absolute without denying the absoluteness of God. The phrase 'the absoluteness of Christianity' therefore contains a fundamental misconception, as if 'Christianity' could assume the place of God as the true Absolute. The Lutheran theologian Carl Heinz Ratschow has therefore called any attempt to claim absoluteness for one's own religion or for any religion the demonization of religion. Our religion, any religion that is claimed to be absolute distracts from the reality of the absolute God.

## 2. The fragmentation of God

From the Christian perspective faith in God, the relationship to the reality of God that is established by God himself through Christ and the Spirit, is therefore the context for understanding and practising interreligious encounter. Christian faith confesses God to be the creator of everything that is not God, the only ground of all being, meaning and truth. This God is believed to be omnipresent, creatively present to his creation at every moment of its existence, omnipotent, the source of all creaturely activity which without God would neither exist nor have effects, and eternal, the giver of all time and the creative beginning and fulfilling end of everything there is. There is always the danger that the universal scope of God's being and act is domesticated through our ecclesial interests and pious sensibilities. We find it easy to see God connected to the church that witnesses, confesses and worships him. But outside the church? It seems natural to see God in the context of the fulfilment of life, of creaturely flourishing, in experiences of happiness and joy. But also in moments of death, in experiences of failure, despair and utter sadness? Many find it easy to believe in a God of grace. But also in a God of judgment? Could it be that the notion of grace becomes empty if it is not the grace that transforms the judgment that would be ours apart from grace? The emphasis on the statement 'God is love' which has correctly been described as the centre of the Christian understanding of God sometimes leads to the tendency to connect God only to our experiences of love and see all other experiences as somehow disconnected from God. Thereby the radical character of God's love which is not only attracted to that which is lovely, but is truly creative in positing the object of his love, truly redemptive by liberating from the absence of love and truly transformative by overcoming that which separates from his love, is denied. In such views there is the danger to transform God almighty, the maker of heaven and earth, into the tribal deity of the Christian church, of turning the God who is love into an idol of our sentimentalism. Such a God, the God of the Christian tribe and of Christian sentiments, is difficult to reconcile with the reality of the religions. There is the danger that the reality of God is restricted to the ecclesial realm and to the sphere of our religious affections. However, in Christian terms this is a denial of God. The tendency to believe in the God of the church, but to assume an attitude of practical atheism to everything outside the church sharply contradicts the biblical insights of the universality of God. Believing in a God who is only present in the church and not in the world, only in the Christian community and not in the religions is a flat denial of faith in God who is the creator and sustainer of the world and who reconciled the world to himself. This God of Christian tribalism and sentimentalism is a fragment of God which renders the whole of the God of faith contradictory. This God is only a God-fragment in a world that is much larger than God.

### 3. Encountering the hiddenness of God: God in the world and God on the cross

If we want to avoid a view that fragments the reality of God by divorcing God from the reality of the religions, how are we to grasp God's presence in the religions more appropriately from the perspective of Christian faith? It might be instructive to follow some of the insights that informed Luther's reflections on the relationship between the God who is hidden in his aweful majesty and the God who has disclosed himself in the suffering of the man on the cross. Luther's theology is an experiential theology that attempts to work through the agonizing tensions that seem to characterize the Christian faith as it is tested again and again by being confronted with the word of scripture. Luther started from a notion of the absolute transcendence of the Divine which we find in the tradition of negative theology exemplified by

Dionysius Areopagita. The way to God is the strenuous ascent of the mystic through the different strata of being to the source of all being, a path that is characterized by a careful denial of all characteristics of created being as they are predicated of God. The mystical logic of negation, a highly rational way of approaching the reality of the Divine, which characterizes for instance Luther's earliest interpretation of the Psalms, the Dictata super Psalterium, is step by step replaced by an existential understanding of the hiddenness of God. Increasingly it is not the absolute transcendence of God above and beyond the world which is the paradigm of God's hiddenness, but the aweful hidden presence of God in everything. If everything that happens in the world, good and evil, joy and suffering, damnation and blessing is to be understood as in some way brought about by God, how are we to relate to the aweful presence of that God? If God is to be God, God cannot be defined from our fragmentary experience of the world. Our experience of the world can be no more than a fragment of the awe-inspiring scope and power of God's activity in everything. This view which is most fully developed in Luther's acerbic dispute with Erasmus of Rotterdam in *On the Bondage of the Will* sees free will only as a divine attribute; in human beings it is a *res de solo titulo*, a mere word that signifies nothing. This view leaves no place for atheism, neither of a theoretical nor of a practical kind, because everything is encompassed and comprehended by the reality of God. Over against that overpowering reality of God it is not the existence of God, but the existence of the world and of humanity that is questionable. It is not the incomprehensibility of the distance of God that is the problem, but the hidden closeness of God in everything that occurs.

While there is no room for atheism in being confronted with this God there is also no room for faith. The reality of God fills everything there is, but it seems to leave no space for a human covenant-partner. The naked majesty of God frustrates all attempts to relate to God. The only way that Luther can point to a liberation from the threatening presence of a God to whom we cannot relate is by means of an inversion of the logic of theological knowledge which finds its clearest expression in the *Heidelberg Disputation* of 1518. The attempt to know God's invisible being through the effects of God will lead to a *theologia gloriae* which sees God as the maximal instantiation of everything that is great, good and powerful in the world. This follows the logic of taking the effects of God's works in the world as fragments which are to be completed in predicating them of God. Against this view Luther asserts: To know God truly is to know God from what becomes visible of God in the world, God's humanity, weakness and foolishness. God is not known by inferring God's character from God's actions but by the disclosure of God's being as it is hidden in the passion of God, the cross of Christ. Luther calls here for an inversion of the logic of knowing God by means of a re-definition of the hiddenness of God. The hiddenness of God by which God discloses his being and becomes visible is the cross of Christ: 'Therefore in Christ crucified there is the true theology and knowledge of God.' We encounter here a radical inversion of the logic of fragmentation and wholeness. Who God really is is disclosed in the hiddenness of God's power and majesty in the suffering of Christ on the cross. The utter fragmentation of Christ's death on the cross discloses who God truly, wholly is. It is here that God relates to us in such a way that we can relate to him, not by relying on the greatness of our moral achievements, but by relying exclusively on the greatness of God's grace which we grasp by unconditional trust in the God who establishes communion with those who on the basis of their own achievements would forever be excluded from God's presence.

It is this hiddenness of God in the cross of Christ that discloses God's true character as creative love that creates eternal life from death, as redeeming love that liberates from the bondage to the powers of destruction and as perfecting love that transforms the fragments of a shattered life into the wholeness of new being. For Luther it is through the cross of Christ that the relationship of faith is established as a faith which trust unconditionally in God's creative righteousness. However, the cross is not an isolated event over against which everything else becomes meaningless. Rather, it discloses the meaning of God's whole story with the world from the beginning of creation to its conclusion in the kingdom of God. It is the point of Jesus' story in which the logic of God's story of humanity is revealed, connecting the story of Israel and the church. The resurrection of the crucified one does not surpass the significance of the God, it declares it. The astonishing fact that the Easter faith of the Christian community did not regard the crucifixion as a last transition through darkness before the light of the Easter morning dawns but summarized its message as 'the message of the cross' (I Cor. 1.18), can only be understood if we share their conviction that the whole of God's story is summarized in the fragmentation of the cross. The message of the cross reveals the God 'who has caused his light to shine in our hearts, the light which is the knowledge of the glory of God in the face of Jesus Christ' (II Cor. 4.6). Only by seeking their orientation from this light Christians can confront the presence of God's majesty in the world. The view of the wholeness of God which they gain from the fragment of the cross of Christ remains fragmentary until the unity of God in Christ, of God, the

Father, the Son and the Spirit, and the God in the world is ultimately disclosed in the kingdom of God. But in this fragment the wholeness of God is already defined in an ultimate way that will not be surpassed by the full disclosure of God in the kingdom.

## Conclusion: lessons for interreligious encounter

What can we gain from this excursion into Luther's agonizing reflections on the two-fold hiddenness of God for the attempt at understanding and practising interreligious encounter in view of the fragmentary experience of God? First of all, it seems clear that from the perspective of Christian faith the religions must be understood theologically. Christians go into inter-religious encounters not with the expectation of moving into godless territory or into lands inhabited by other deities. If they believe that God is the omnipresent, omnipotent and eternal creator and sustainer of everything they will expect to encounter the presence of God in other religions. To exclude the religions from the scope of God's activity denies central attributes of the God the church confesses as the Father, the Son and the Holy Spirit. Other religions are therefore not human creations as if a Feuerbachian theory of projection could be applied to all religions apart from Christianity. They are part of God's ways with the world. Christians will, however, have to acknowledge that the presence of God in the religions is hidden to them. It has not been revealed to them, because the revelation in which Christian faith is grounded is the knowledge of the glory of God in the face of Christ. It is from this perspective that Christian faith has to try to understand the hidden presence of God in the religions.

Secondly, Christians who are willing to learn from Luther's relocation of the disclosure of God's being in the fragmentation of Christ's death on the cross will not expect that somehow their fragmentary experience of God and the fragmentary experiences of God in other religions adds up to a holistic vision of God, a global concept of God that only needs to be pieced together by skilful theologians until the pattern of the true character of God begins to appear from the puzzle. That would only be a new *theologia gloriae* in global perspective. Before the *eschaton* there is for Christians no other way than to hold on to the fragmentary experience of the glory of God on the face of the crucified one as the disclosure of God's glory under its opposite. However, Christian faith commits those to whom the knowledge of God's glory has been disclosed in the face of Christ to the belief that the cross of Christ is the content of the message of God's reconciliation with the world, a reconciliation which is grounded in God's grace and not in the agreement of parties in conflict.

Thirdly, Christians who see the fragment of the cross as the ground of faith's insight into God's being will have their attention redirected to seek the manifestation of God not in the awe-inspiring presence of the majesty of God but in the vulnerability and fragility of human lives threatened by injustice and destruction, in fragmented lives rather than in the glory of power. A Christian witness in interreligious encounters that is informed by the revelation of God in the suffering of the cross will have to share this God's preference for widows and orphans, for those suffering injustice and violence, because it is in the injustice of a violent death that God chose to disclose his love and his justice as a creative love that creates community where there was hatred and offers reconciliation where there was enmity. If Christians can perceive the wholeness of God, the unity of the God of Christ, the Father, the Son and the Spirit and of the hiddenness of God in the world, including God's hidden presence in the religions, only in the fragment of the cross of Christ, their witness in interreligious encounter must be shaped by this disclosure of God in such a way that the protest against unjust suffering, the attempt to overcome the violence that destroys peaceful relations between cultures and religions, will be the context in which the text of the Christian witness makes sense. From this perspective it would contradict the content of the Christian message, if interreligious encounters were turned into a power-struggle of different religious truth-claims, the exchange of competing theologies of glory. Witnessing to the truth of the gospel remains bound to the context of the gospel as a message of liberation and comfort for those who are weary and whose load is heavy (Matt.11.28). All too often the Christian insistence on the truth has distorted the character of the gospel and has been presented as a new law and not as a message of liberation. The criticism of other religions which will have to be expressed in interreligious dialogue where religions stand in the way of justice, peace and human flourishing will only be credible if it is accompanied by a profound self-criticism of Christians where they have falsified the truth they claim to witness in the way they have expressed it, in word and in deed. The christological criterion which shapes the engagement of Christians in interreligious encounter places all dialogue about religious truth-claims in the context of a shared striving of all involved in such dialogue for the flourishing of human lives in all its personal and social dimensions.

Finally, in the perspective of faith all interreligious encounters are placed in an eschatological horizon of the coming of the kingdom where the truth of God will be evident for all to see because God has brought about the perfect communion with his reconciled creation. The final perfection of the beatific vision and the final judgment of all claims to truth by the disclosure of the unity of all truth in God may not be presumed upon – neither in the practice of Christian faith nor by theories of interreligious encounter. Presuming upon God is the very character of sin. We remain in the realm of the fragmentary, confronted by the hiddenness of God, but assured that in the midst of fragmentation, God has disclosed his truth in the cross of Christ. For Christians this and nothing else holds the promise that we are on the way towards the disclosure of the wholeness of God where God himself will draw away the veil of hiddenness so that we will see the unity of the Father, the Son and the Spirit, which we now believe in, with the God whose hidden presence in the world now challenges and questions faith in its deepest tribulations. The way of Christian believers through history encountering other believers on the way, engaging them in conversation and co-operation for the good of God's creation, is like the mystical path, a journey through the darkness of the hiddenness of God, but comforted and assured that the grace and truth of God which we can now only grasp in the fragmentary mirror of the theology of the cross will be revealed as God's own theology of glory.

## Further reading

Martin Luther, *The Bondage of the Will* (1526) in *Luther's Works*, Vol. 33, Philadelphia: Concordia/Fortress, 2nd edn 1977, pp.15–295.

Martin Luther, *Heidelberg Disputation* in *Luther's Works*, Vol. 31, Philadelphia: Concordia/Muhlenberg 1957, pp. 39–70.

Albrecht Peters, 'Verborgener Gott – dreieiniger Gott nach Martin Luther' in Karl Rahner (ed), *Der eine und der dreiene Gott. Das Gottesverständnis bei Christen, Juden und Muslimen*, Zürich: Benzinger 1983, pp.117–40.

Carl Heinz Ratschow, *Die Religionen. Handbuch Systematischer Theologie*, Vol. 16, Gütersloh: Gütersloher Verlagshaus 1981.

Carl Heinz Ratschow, 'Rechtfertigung. Diakritisches Prinzip des Christentums im Verhältnis zu den anderen Religionen' in ibid., *Von den Wandlungen Gottes. Beiträge zur Systematischen Theologie*, Berlin/New York: de Gruyter 1986, pp.336–75.

Christoph Schwöbel, 'Particularity, Universality and the Religions. Toward a Christian Theology of Religions' in Gavin D'Costa (ed), *Christian Uniqueness Reconsidered. The Myth of a Pluralistic Theology of Religions*, New York: Orbis 1990, pp.30–46.

Christoph Schwöbel, 'Die Wahrheit des Glaubens im religiös-weltanschaulichen Pluralismis' in Ulrich Kühn, Michael Markert, Matthias Petzoldt (eds), *Christlicher Wahrheitsanspruch zwischen Fundamentalismus und Pluralität*, Leipzig: Evangelische Verlagsanstalt 1998, pp.88–118.

# Revelation and the Trinitarian Concept of God: Are they Key Concepts for Theological Thought?

At present the concept of the Trinity is playing a key role in theological thought and thus seems to be replacing revelation in its prime place as the first principle of theological thinking. In this article I want to assess the significance of both concepts for present-day theology.

## I. Revelation as a key concept of theology after Vatican II

Christian faith confesses the revelation of God in history and in so doing testifies that any real experience of God can be communicated only through God. We human beings have no direct grasp of God because as human beings we are God's creatures. Thus to speak of the revelation of God always already means a recognition of the radical difference between God the creator and God's creatures, and at the same time also a recognition of the possibility of being able to attain a knowledge of God, however fragmentary, through corresponding intermediaries in the fellowship of believers. So our knowledge of God does not rest on the brilliant contribution of individual Christians but on the self-revelation of God attested in the church of Jesus Christ: God's self-revelation has taken place both in the history of Israel and in the preaching, the crucifixion and resurrection of Jesus, whom in the fellowship of Christians we confess to be the Son of God. Hence finally the whole of God's creation will be experienced and interpreted as a testimony to the divine self-revelation.

Accordingly, it is not difficult to distinguish at least three forms of the communication of revelation in the Christian church: Bible, tradition and church. These three vehicles are intimately connected, in that the Bible is itself part of tradition and the tradition is shaped dynamically in the fellowship of believers.

Thus to call Christianity a religion of revelation does not mean so much pointing to individual experiences of men and women in history here and there as having a transcendent foundation, but rather saying that Christian faith derives totally from God through grace. The special relationship between God and human beings that we call grace thus has its basis in God's will to communicate Godself to his creatures, and in the affirmative response of believers to God it becomes living and dynamic reality and transforming power. Thus Christian faith derives from the divine dynamic of revelation as a whole and not from some perceptions of individuals with particularly 'supernatural' gifts. The human response to God's revelation is shaped by the personal Yes to God within the living fellowship of believers.

Whereas Vatican I developed the theological foundations of this understanding of revelation in terms of teaching about a deposit of truths, Vatican II attempted to understand the divine revelation as a real personal self-communication by God to us human beings. The accent thus shifted from an understanding of revelation which was more in terms of teaching and instruction to a more personal and soteriological understanding of divine revelation which emphasizes the invitation to all men and women to participate in the divine nature.[1] Revelation is accordingly less a cognitive event than an eschatological event which grants access to the Father for all men and women through Christ, the incarnate Word, in the Holy Spirit. Jesus Christ is at the same time both the mediator and the fullness of the whole of revelation (*Dei Verbum* 2).

Thus the understanding of revelation propagated by Vatican II reaches substantially further than that of Vatican I. Revelation is no longer so closely identified with doctrinal decisions, but is regarded as a dynamic saving event, so that the deeper connection between world history, the Bible and Christian tradition can be seen. God's self-communication is effective in human history from the beginning and is perceived by the different religious currents of humankind, in however fragmentary a way. It can be concluded from this that it is illegitimate to declare God's presence to be the sole possession of a particular tradition. Dialogue between the religions, which was so clearly supported by Vatican II (cf. *Nostra aetate* 2), is also inspired by this understanding of revelation.

This brief look at the changes in the understanding of revelation within the Roman Catholic tradition makes clear the movements to which the concept of revelation has been exposed down to our day. Each of them requires a clear conceptual definition. At present at least four understandings of revelation exist side by side in Christian terminology and they are often interwoven:

*1. The understanding of revelation as epiphany.* This has been developed from antiquity down to our day and indicates the possibility that any phenomenon in our world can become the vehicle of a revelation, the moment for the disclosure of the holy. Mircea Eliade develops his concept of hierophany in this connection. He argues that there is no break in continuity from the most elementary hierophany, e.g. the manifestation of the holy in an ordinary object, a stone or a tree, to the highest hierophany (which for Christians is the incarnation of God in Jesus Christ). In each case we experience the same mysterious process: the manifestation of something from a quite different order, a reality which does not belong to our world, in the objects which are completely part of our natural 'profane' world.[2] Paul Ricoeur and David Tracy have developed further this understanding of revelation as manifestation.[3]

*2. The theoretical understanding of revelation as instruction.* This attempts to communicate knowledge of God's self-revelation in clearly formulated doctrinal statements. On the one hand this intellectual treatment of revelation is a necessary process in the church, and on the other it constantly runs the risk of reducing revelation to the doctrinal information that it contains, thus separating the event of revelation from the saving event.[4] 'The mysteries of faith are brought down to the level of supernatural mysteries of understanding and the virtue of faith lies in obediently holding obscure *veritates revelatae* to be true.'[5]

*3. A reductionist understanding of revelation* has influenced religious thought from the time of the Enlightenment onwards. Revelation is the sign of an epoch of humankind which is not yet enlightened. In his work *The Education of the Human Race*, Lessing explains how truths once revealed are to be taken over into truths of reason, for 'the shaping of revealed truths into truths of reason is absolutely necessary if the human race is to be helped by them. When they were revealed, of course they were not as yet truths of religion; but they were revealed to be so. They were as it were the result which the mathematics teacher gives his pupils first, so that they can be to some degree guided by it in their calculations' (section 76).[6]

Revelation comes rightly into its own only in human reason. Biblical texts project a truth which ultimately can be arrived at by human reason itself. So in a future age of human existence people would no longer need a revelation, but could rely entirely on human reason.

The Christian concept of revelation must guard against at least two reductions: first a reduction to the mere content of teaching, and secondly a reduction of historical revelation to mere reason. Moreover, both reductions are connected, to the degree that the theoretical concept of revelation in terms of instruction was an attempt to provide an apologetic counter to the reductionism of the Enlightenment.

*4. A relational understanding of revelation* is presented by Vatican II. According to this, the divine revelation is not aimed at the disclosure of this or that thing but relates to God's self-communication to us men and women. It is about the salvation of all men and women. So revelation is not given in order to depict God's being within the Trinity to humankind, but to realize God's plan of salvation, God's living relationship to us: 'It pleased God, in his goodness and wisdom, to reveal himself and to make known the mystery of his will . . . that men should have access to the Father, through Christ, the word made flesh, in the Holy Spirit, and thus become sharers in the divine nature' (*Dei verbum* 2). God's saving will can be experienced in the encounter with Holy Scripture: 'It follows that all the preaching of the Church, as indeed the entire Christian religion, should be nourished and ruled by sacred Scripture' (*Dei verbum* 21).

So a critical concept of Christian revelation must do justice to at least the following conditions: the relationship between revelation and faith, the relationship between faith and reason, the relationship between God and God's self-revelation in human history communicated by Christian tradition and the possible revelation of God in other traditions, the relationship between revelation as gift and revelation as the task of interpretation, the relationship between revelation and truth, and the relationship between revelation and human salvation. Thus the concept of revelation is beyond dispute a central concept in the network of theological thinking.

It is therefore quite consistent that in the period after Vatican II there should have been a discussion of revelation as what Eicher has called a 'principle of modern theology'.[7] Revelation was meant to help to provide a basis for the identity of Christian faith and thus also of Christian theology. One of the functions of the concept of revelation was to unite.[8] No wonder, then, that the theology of the 1970s and 1980s was intensively preoccupied with hermeneutical questions. In this way the communicative form of the event of revelation was to be investigated more precisely.

However, theological interest increasingly shifted in the middle of the 1980s. The concept of revelation and the hermeneutical treatment of the event of revelation no longer occupied the forefront of theological attention, but the trinitarian concept of God.

## II. The trinitarian concept of God as a key term in post-modern theological thought

The many books about God which have appeared in recent years also contain discussions of God's mysterious being, which are concerned to rehabilitate apophatic theology. But the main focus of theological literature is the trinitarian concept of God. More than fifty books on the trinitarian concept of God have appeared from Western publishers in the last fifteen years, not to mention the countless articles on the same theme in professional theological journals. So theological interest has clearly moved from a discussion of the event of divine revelation to a discussion of the divine being.[9]

Among the variety of motives which lie behind this new interest in God's being on the part of Christian theology are the quest for Christian identity in a pluralistic religious context and the attempt to derive direct help in the orientation of Christian praxis from a concept of God which has clear profiles. Of course other factors also play an important role, like the attempt to progress to a more critical concept of God in the face of feminist criticism of the traditional concept of God and the attempt to develop afresh through a discussion of divine 'persons' the concept of subject which has become so unsure in post-modernity.[10]

As once happened with the concept of revelation, so today the concept of God is assuming an increasingly more central role in the quest for models of Christian praxis and teaching. This sheds clearer light on the close connection between the understanding of God and human action. But at the same time new ideological strains on the concept of God are coming into view which call for corresponding strategies of theological self-criticism.

I want to discuss these connections in more detail, using the two-fold discussion of the dialogue between the religions and the trinitarian concept of God as a example. In his most recent book, *The Meeting of Religions and the Trinity*, Gavin D'Costa pursues three aims. First of all he wants to put in question the customary distinction between exclusivism, inclusivism and pluralism in the Christian theology of the religions. Secondly, he emphasizes that every theology is bound to a tradition. And thirdly, he develops an inter-religious dialogue programme in terms of an exclusivist trinitarianism. With the help of this he hopes to master all the problems in the theology of religions from a Christian perspective.[11]

In connection with his first concern, D'Costa sets out to show that the pluralistic theologies of religion put forward by John Hick and Paul Knitter are untenable. D'Costa makes the usual charges against Hick's thesis that all religions are on the way to the same reality, and against Knitter's thesis that all religions are to be measured by the degree to which they seek ecological and human justice and prosperity. In his view, Hick makes an unhistorical generalization which leaves out the really difficult distinctions between the religions and is based on a mythologizing hermeneutics, and Knitter forces the religions, each of which has a distinctive character, into an ethical strait-jacket which has been constructed in advance. Thus Knitter is said to state what right religious and ethical praxis is even before the real dialogue between the religions. Finally, both pluralists are said to suffer from an exclusivism of revelation which does not perceive the real concerns and experiences of the individual religions. So the project of religious pluralism is said to rest on an exclusivist Kantian modernism and like this is doomed to failure.

But D'Costa also has charges to lay against inclusivism. On closer examination this turns out to be concealed exclusivism. For the advocates of a Christian inclusivism do not succeed in endorsing other religions as a way to salvation. One cannot affirm just some parts of a religious tradition and deny others which do not correspond to one's own tradition. Inclusivists, therefore, do not respect the integrity of another religion. In reality they may be eclectic or weaker exclusivists, but they are still exclusivists.

At this point D'Costa emphasizes that any position in the theology of religion is exclusivist in one way or another, so that the whole typology must be given up. Rather, he wants to show that a trinitarian meta-narrative is pre-eminently suitable for narrating an unfinished history in respect of the other religions and at the same time allowing other religions their own voice.[12] So he wants to develop a Christian theology of religion by means of the trinitarian concept of God.

D'Costa points to the indissoluble connection between Bible, tradition and magisterium and discusses various church documents since *Nostra Aetate* (1965). He sees the connection between a theology of the Holy Spirit and the trinitarian presence of God in other religions and cultures as being clarified above all in *Redemptoris Missio* (1991).[13] This presence of the triune God in the other cultures represents an internal challenge to Christians to reflect self-critically on their own tradition and the ecclesiological forms which express it.[14] D'Costa also repeatedly emphasizes the indissoluble relationship between Trinity and ecclesiology.[15] Finally, it becomes quite clear that in D'Costa's thought the Trinity becomes the theological presupposition and only valid criterion of theology and inter-religious encounter. Here the Trinity takes on the status of a transcendental condition for inter-religious dialogue.[16]

On the basis of his concept of tradition, which is inspired by Alasdair MacIntyre, D'Costa seeks and finds his orientation for the encounter with other religions in Roman Catholic theology of the Trinity. Here it is striking that D'Costa is not concerned either about the discussion of the nature and changing of tradition or about the discussion of the various models of trinitarian thought within Roman Catholic theology which has taken place in various theological schemes since Vatican II, for example in feminist theology.

In feminist theology, tradition does not prove to be an innocent process of the continuous handing-on of Christian faith which can guide our thought rightly; rather, it is a process which from the perspective of Christian women contains elements of both oppression and liberation and therefore requires a critical and self-critical hermeneutics and critique of ideology. The conflict between the so-called revolutionary feminists and the so-called reforming feminists turns on this very evaluation: is the Christian tradition so hopelessly patriarchal that we can no longer expect from it any stimuli towards the liberation of believers for the power of gender constructions that have been forced on them? Or in the Christian tradition itself are there experiences of liberation which are essential for the formation of authentic Christian theology and praxis?[17]

These important questions cannot be settled simply by D'Costa's reference to the fact that theology is situated within a particular tradition. Rather, so-called reforming feminism is concerned to understand, to explain and to interpret self-critically the Christian tradition, with the aim of helping to play a part in shaping this tradition constructively. That means that theology needs a critical hermeneutic which gives clear methodological orientation to this process of shaping tradition. This methodological orientation must not be undermined thematically by a particular concept of God, nor even by reference to the transcendental role of the concept of God. Years ago, Karl Rahner warned against misusing the authority of God for every possible human project.[18]

From the beginning the close connection between the Christian concept of God and the shaping of Christian tradition has been emphasized and discussed critically in feminist theology. So we can see why prominent theologians like Elizabeth Johnson and Catherine LaCugna have been particularly preoccupied with the trinitarian concept of God.[19]

Elizabeth Johnson points out that women's quest for less inappropriate ways of talking of God is meeting up today with other theological attempts to reconsider the doctrine of God which has been inherited, the expression of which has itself been in a crisis of expression for some time.[20] In her contribution to a reformulation of the trinitarian mystery Johnson immediately recognizes that the exclusive use of male images is the first difficulty that emerges when the Trinity is discussed from a feminist perspective[21] and that other systems of metaphors are needed which can demonstrate the equality, opposition and reciprocal dynamic in the relationships within the Trinity.[22] Furthermore, for Johnson it is important to see that the difference between the trinitarian schemes is an advantage and not a disadvantage. So Johnson's own attempt to understand God as Sophia-God is intrinsically no more and no less than such a contribution to a discussion which needs to be taken further.[23] However, for Johnson it is indispensable that at the heart of the sacred mystery there is not monarchy but fellowship, not an absolute ruler but threefold koinonia.[24] Johnson does not think naively that she can grasp the mystery of all relationship. Rather, she is in search of new concepts which can better express the divine quality of relationship, which is worshipped and proclaimed in the mystery of the Trinity.

Unfortunately Johnson does not investigate the connection between the dialogue between religions and the quest for appropriate concepts of God. However, she does endorse the critical function of the symbol of the Trinity – here in the face of patriarchal domination in the church and society, which is rooted in the fact that the image of God is the final point of reference for the values of a society.[25]

This brief look at feminist theology has shown that, as also happens in D'Costa, though in different terms, here too the connection between Christian tradition, the image of God and readiness for theological dialogue is recognized. But whereas for D'Costa the Christian tradition is an unproblematical starting point and the trinitarian concept of God becomes the unambiguous basis of inter-religious dialogue, in feminist theology the two cornerstones of theological thinking emphatically become a problem, though they also take on their own dynamic.

For our context, this means on the one hand that a theology open to dialogue between the religions may not prescribe for itself either an uncritical concept of tradition or an uncritical trinitarian system, and on the other that in an authentic dialogue with those of other faiths and other ways of thinking new and perhaps surprising insights into one's own process of tradition and one's own thinking and speaking about God must be reckoned with. Even from within, i.e. from one's own Christian logic, a trinitarian and traditionalistic exclusivism is unacceptable.

However, this is not to dispute either D'Costa's criticism of Hick and Knitter's religious pluralism or the connection between the concept of God and the dialogue between religions, to which D'Costa has drawn attention. Rather, the problems, and also the dynamic, of these problems has become clearer.

## III. Revelation and the concept of God

Our discussion has shown that neither revelation nor the Trinity can function as unproblematical key concepts for theological thought. Both concepts have ideological connotations and must therefore be exposed to a critical hermeneutic. They are not suitable as the exclusive vehicles for theological schemes. Nether concept provides an untroubled theological orientation and an unambiguous pattern for Christian identity in our complex world of religious diversity. Rather, both concepts are already results of the interpretation of Christian experience in history. Here revelation emphasizes more the process of the self-communication of God and the Trinity emphasizes the origin of Christian revelation in the triune God. It is important not only to emphasize the character of the two concepts as experience but also not to neglect the christological, sotierological and eschatological character of Christian faith by looking for theological orientation by means of key concepts. The dialectic between christology and thought about the Trinity must not be dissolved. God's self-communication or the relations within God are of interest to us human beings precisely because of their character as claim and promise: in Jesus Christ the one God invites us human beings to a loving relationship with God in God's creation.

It is the same God who is also worshipped by Jews and Muslims. A trinitarian exclusivism therefore runs the risk of reducing God to a Christian tribal God, while a relativistic pluralism (such as we find in John Hick) criminally neglects the concrete character of revelation to be found in all belief in God and tries to do away with it in an unfounded universalism.[26]

In our culture and time, too, theology has the task of shedding light critically and self-critically on the sphere of Christian faith and thought. In this sphere there are not only other religions but also diverse attempts to live out the truth of the Christian revelation of God in the church and to disclose it intellectually. The Christian traditions, texts and doctrinal decisions provide orientation in this process. Theology works out strategies for interpreting tradition and strategies of dialogue with all Christians and non-Christians who are interested in a reciprocally critical discussion of God's self-revelation in human history.[27] Moreover, it seeks characteristics of Christian identity in the diversity of religious manifestations.

But as God's mystery can never be exhausted by human beings, even by believers, Christian identity too can in the last resort only be thought of inclusively, i.e. in an *a priori* open and self-critical way. This does not mean a weak identity, but an identity which always already understands itself as task, because it receives its energy from its centre of revelation and not by exclusively guarding its outermost frontiers.

*Translated by John Bowden*

## Notes

1. Cf. Josef Schmitz, 'Das Christentum als Offenbarungsreligion im kirchlichen Bekenntnis' in W. Kern, H. J. Pottmeyer and Max Seckler (eds), *Handbuch der Fundamentaltheologie 2, Traktat Offenbarung*, Tübingen and Basel, 2nd edn 2000, pp.1–12.
2. Mircea Eliade, *The Sacred and the Profane: The Nature of Religion*, New York and London 1959, p.11.
3. See Paul Ricoeur, *Figuring the Sacred: Religion, Narrative, and the Sacred*, Minneapolis 1995, ch. 2; David Tracy, *The Analogical Imagination: Christian Theology and the Culture of Pluralism*, New York and London 1981, ch. 3; id., *Dialogue with the Other: The Inter-Religious Dialogue*, Louvain 1990, p.43. See also Werner G. Jeanrond, 'The Significance of Revelation for Biblical Theology', *Biblical Interpretation* 6, 1998, pp.243–57.
4. Cf. Max Seckler, 'Der Begriff der Offenbarung' in *Handbuch der Fundamentaltheologie* 2 (n.1), pp.41–61.
5. Ibid., p.46.
6. Quoted from *Lessings Werke in fünf Bänden* 2, Berlin and Weimar, seventh edn 1975, p.311.
7. Peter Eicher, *Offenbarung: Prinzip neuzeitlicher Theologie*, Munich 1977.
8. Ibid., pp.584–86.
9. Of course considerable theological energy continues to be devoted to the concept of revelation, but there is no mistaking the fact that the concept of the Trinity has overtaken the concept of revelation in terms of theological interest.

More recent books on the concept of revelation include Colin E. Gunton, *A Brief Theology of Revelation*, Edinburgh 1995; Hans Waldenfels, *Einführung in die Theologie der Offenbarung*, Darmstadt 1996; Paul Avis (ed), *Divine Revelation*, London 1997.

10. These and other interests in theological discussion of the Trinity are documented e.g. in the following volumes: James M. Byrne (e.), *The Christian Understanding of God Today*, Dublin 1993; Christoph Schwöbel (ed), *Trinitarian Theology Today*, Edinburgh 1995; Stephen Davies, Daniel Kendall and Gerald O'Collins (eds), *The Trinity*, Oxford 1999.

11. Gavin D'Costa, *The Meeting of Religions and the Trinity*, Maryknoll, NY 2000.

12. Ibid., p.92.

13. Ibid., p.114: 'Hence, it is clear and unambiguous that through the Spirit, God's trinitarian presence within other religions and cultures is a possibility, and one that is discerned by signs of the kingdom inchoately present within that culture.'

14. Ibid., p.115: 'If the Spirit is at work in the religions, then the gifts of the Spirit need to be discovered, fostered, and received into the church. If the church fails to be receptive, it may be unwittingly practising cultural and religious idolatry.'

15. See ibid., pp.121ff.

16. In this connection see also Kevin Vanhoozer (ed), *The Trinity in a Pluralistic Age*, Grand Rapids 1997, pp.41–71.

17. Cf. Valarie H. Ziegler, 'Tradition' in L. M. Russell and J. S. Clarkson (eds), *Dictionary of Feminist Theologies*, London 1996, pp.301–2.

18. See Karl Rahner, 'Autorität' in *Christlicher Glaube in moderner Gesellschaft* 14, Freiburg, Basel and Vienna 1982, pp.8f.

19. Catherine Mowry LaCugna, *God for Us: The Trinity and Human Life*, San Francisco 1991; Elizabeth A. Johnson, *She Who Is: The Mystery of God in Feminist Theological Discourse*, New York 1992.

20. Johnson, *She Who Is*, p.19.

21. Ibid., p.193.

22. Ibid., p.197.

23. In ibid., p.221, Johnson points out that ultimately it becomes clear that just one way of speaking is never appropriate.

24. Ibid., p.216.

25. Ibid., p.223.

26. Cf. Gavin Flood, *Beyond Phenomenology: Rethinking the Study of Religion*, London and New York 1999, p.56: 'To disclaim in a totalizing way that all traditions are paths leading to the same goal is to disclaim their uniqueness.'

27. See Werner G. Jeanrond, *Theological Hermeneutics: Development and Significance*, London 1994.

# Images, Icons and Idols of God: The Question of Truth in Christian Theology

### JOSEPH MOINGT

The theological question of truth which is raised by the distinction between 'images, icons and idols' essentially relates to conceptual representations of God. An etymological reference to the Greek words *eikon* or *eidolon* or to the Latin *imago* does not help us to distinguish between these three terms, since they are all capable of bearing the same meanings: portrait, reflection, imitation, likeness, idea, imagination – but also a deceitful counterpart, an erroneous imitation, an illusion, a phantom. Generally speaking, theological usage has attached to 'idol' the pejorative senses that the two other words could bear. Do we need to distinguish between these two other words further? A quite recent specific usage, in philosophy, theology and art, favours icon as the opposite of idol, so that image can become a neutral word: it is either iconic or idolatrous, i.e. true or false (false in the sense of illusory or deceitful). Alternatively, it takes on an intermediate value and is reduced to being the visible support of representation; in that case the tacit pre-supposition is that the simple image runs the risk of being degraded to an idol if it does not succeed in directing the gaze beyond the realm of the senses. The basic question of truth, which goes back to the very origin of theology, is whether one should *a priori* mistrust the sensual nature of the image (and thus also of language).

## I. The icon

### *1. The icon repels the idol*

Jean-Luc Marion has analysed the philosophical and theological significance of the icon as opposed to the idol (in a way which is more theological than philosophical):[1] the idol imposes itself, it stands out, it attracts the attention, it focusses the gaze on itself in a sensual way, it cannot be avoided or passed over, nor does it direct attention towards the invisible reality which it claims to represent. Rather, it absorbs the divine into itself; it imprisons it to the degree that the human gaze can bear, i.e. see. This is the case with concepts of God developed from the idea of being in Plato, Aristotle, Thomas Aquinas and Kant up to the point where they have been denied (fortunately) by Nietzsche and Heidegger. By contrast, the icon simply allows the divine to appear[2] and withdraws, so that the invisible may arise without being fixed in the visible: it opens up on a countenance which directs the human gaze towards 'the invisible gaze which it visibly envisages', in such a way that the eye sees the visible as the invisible sees it: with the senses so withdrawn that the authentic concepts of the divine can be revealed.

This conception is manifestly inspired by Orthodox theology,[3] according to which the icon, illuminated from within, 'gives rise to a personal presence', leads towards transcendence clothed in a 'mystical and quasi-sacramental value'.[4] In language which is both theological and pictorial, the painter and theologian Léonide Ouspensky explains that when the idol  *icon* represents Christ or a saint or a biblical scene, it does not seek to be the portrait of an ordinary man or simply depict a historical or natural scene. It sets out to be the 'revelation of eternity in time', to suggest the human vocation of deification, to express 'the spiritual experience of holiness',[5] to make the grace which consumes nature shine through. It does not seek to represent divinity but the participation of the human in the divine; it seeks to give an image of the divine beauty, to refer back to the invisible reality which transfixes the visible. It does not reflect the individual vision of the artist but the teaching of the church which inspires its gaze; thus icons are above all icons of Christ, the art of which flows from the dogma of the incarnation.

## 2. The icon is abstracted from the image

It is here that the difference appears between the icon, as it has just been described, and the image, as it is conceived of and practised in Western Christian art. As the author himself emphasizes, this is quite a radical one. Thus Russian or Byzantine iconography is not interested in representing a particular scene from the life of Christ in its historical reality or the suffering humanity of Christ apprehended in the natural features of the human condition; it is interested, rather, in his 'divino-humanity', his flesh bearing the glory of the deity. Again we find the same distance between such a Russian icon of the Virgin and the Child and Raphael's Madonna of the Grand Duke as that which separates the unique divine Motherhood from all other human motherhood.[6] Disapproved of though it may be, the Western sacred *image* is not denounced as an *idol*; however, it is clear that it does not attain the theological truth of the icon because of its attachment to the visible.

So that is the question of truth that we have to examine. For through art it is the intellectual representation of divine and 'supernatural' realities which is at issue: the analogical knowledge of God through created per-fections, the value of the biblical metaphors which are immersed in the realm of the senses; the scope of the dogmatic concepts which again have the same origin. To put it more broadly, the issue is that of the constitution of theological discourse, of its orientation and its interest. Granted that it has to 'convert itself' from the visible to the invisible in order to express God, the question is one of knowing at what point it can and should withdraw from what is purely human, natural and temporal. But what would be the truth for us of a discourse about God detached from all that makes up human reality?

## II. The image

### *1. Two images in one*

Now scripture has chosen the way of the image for us. It is true that for scripture every image that is made of God is tainted with idolatry; the pro-hibition against images, which lay at the heart of the iconoclastic crisis, does not interest us as such. The Bible presents no less than two images of God which it makes; these are put in creation, the world of the senses, as two places or two means of revelation and knowledge of God's divinity. The two images are the human being created man and woman in God's likeness and the man Jesus Christ his Son. It what way are they both images, and in what way can we use them to arrive at proper representations of God? These are the terms in which I shall raise the question of truth, and I want to respond to them by showing that truth is truth about God only with reference to these two images, which are themselves always referred to each other.

One might ask whether it is permissible to put them side by side as if they had the same weight of truth: every divine representation taken from the human image could only lead to idolatry, and that has in fact happened. That is the reason for the biblical prohibition. Christ alone is image of God because he is God in person, and human beings attain to the dignity of the image only to the extent of their union with Christ. That is the basis of the theology of the icon, but if we follow this reasoning through to the end there is true knowledge of God only in Christ – a thesis which cannot be sustained in the absolute. Christ *can* reveal God because he comes from God, but it is because he belongs integrally to the human species and human history that he reveals *effectively* that 'God is for us' (Rom. 8.31) and that he is for us, and it is in this way that he is the image of God in his historical nature. Conversely, it is because human beings are predestined to fulfil themselves in Christ that they are open to transcendence, and it is in that way that they are also the image of God in this very nature. The two images make a hermeneutical circle, one taking direction from the other, one unfolding itself in the other in such a way as to make them only one, but in a difference which is maintained. The truth of every divine representation depends on the bipolarity of this unique and total image.

## 2. *The human image*

In the most immediate biblical sense, it seems that the human being is the image of God (or in the image, or in the likeness of God – it does not much matter here) by virtue of the 'lordly' power which has been given him to have dominion over the earth and to impose a name on all living beings, and also by virtue of the freedom implied by this lordship, which sets human beings apart from other creatures, though dependent on the creator who delegates his power to them. So the human being is an image for the same reason that he is bound to creation, related to it, responsible for it. It is by his body, which is his being in the world, that he exercises this charge. That affects first of all the other who is like him. The statement 'man and woman created he them', attached to the story of the creation of Eve from the flesh of Adam, shows us that the sexual nature of human beings, understood as their relationship to one another, is not alien to the image of God. They are the image of God in their bodies as well. The responsibility which is entrusted to them for his world and for their like, which bears no comparison to the desire of each to live for himself, is the first revelation of this infinite otherness which is the divine fatherhood towards every creature.

The church fathers, reflecting that God is an incorporeal spirit, would say later that man is not in the image of God according to his corporeal nature but according to his spiritual nature, in that he is endowed with intelligence and will, is capable of knowing and loving God, and is destined to see God; they also asked what has happened to this image as a result of original sin. They accept that it has been 'soiled' 'disfigured', but never completely lost; it has then been 'restored' by the grace of Christ, and the likeness becomes increasingly great through being worked on by grace. These corrections and precisions, legitimate as they are, can be explained by the anthropology of past centuries; they always nevertheless presuppose that the image of God, which is the anchorage of the supernatural vocation of human beings, is inserted in their nature as a basic fact of the human condition, which present-day anthropology defines in terms of corporeality and temporality.

So we could concede that human beings succeed in being fully the *icon* of God only by the transformation which grace brings about in them, but we will maintain that they are formally the *image* of God by virtue of the historic destiny which confers on them the charge of humanizing their like and working towards a more human world. This destiny is the sense which orientates human history towards Christ in whom it will be fulfilled; reciprocally, it also orientates the preformation of the humanity of Christ in this same history which can be read, retrospectively, as a history of salvation.

Thus the human image receives its significance by anticipation from Christ, and the Christic image receives its effective visibility from the historic heritage that it assumes. It follows that discourse about God shows its truth only if it *also* speaks of human beings in terms of their own world. It is in this world, as in a mirror, that the transcendental vocation of humanity must be deployed: the image, the reflection of the transcendent problem which raises it up, draws it on and already inhabits it, through even the contradiction of sin. To talk truly about God is not to speak the truth about God in himself, which is inaccessible to us, but to speak the truth about our relationship with God: not only about the vocation of the immortal soul to the eternal vision of God, since that immediately ends up in idealism, but about the relationship of God to our natural and historical world, the truth of which is revealed in the man Jesus also under the inverse mode of the relationship of God to us.

## 3. The Christic image

If we now consider in what way Christ is the image of God, we do so not solely to develop a christological point, but again to determine how the reference to Christ provides a criterion of truth for all our representations of God. We again begin from iconic theology, which takes as its model the scene of the transfiguration of Christ: the glory of the divinity of the incarnate Word, going through and illuminating the opacity of the flesh, is transparent in its humanity, making the presence of the invisible recognizable there.[7] That is true, but this is a theophany, like that at the burning bush; in other words an appearance of God himself, who makes himself miraculously visible. Where then is the image, strictly speaking, since it is supposed to be distinct from the reality of which it is the reflection? One could conceive of it as being the flesh of Christ illuminated and set on fire by the divine glory. That is again true, but it would not be this image by itself, according to its human nature; it would be so only through a transforming action which withdrew it from its creaturely condition, as an instrument moved by the deity. This would again be transitory and expressed in an event, evident to some rare persons who were themselves illuminated by a divine favour. It would not be accessible to just anyone. At best, the humanity of Jesus would be the mirror in which there appeared, not an image, but the radiance of divinity; not a reflection of a distant reality but something that arose from his presence there. Is this truly the way in which Christ is the image of God? It is clear what is at issue with this question. According to this 'Taborite' reference the only true discourse about God would be pure mystical contemplation, at the limits of ecstatic rapture,[8] with no relation to the earthly and historical condition of the human being except to snatch him away after the fashion of the transfigured Christ.

Let us turn to the New Testament to find an answer to our question. We must look for it in the totality of the manifestation of Christ rather than in the exegesis of the few very rare texts where he is called 'image of God', an expression which itself relates to the totality of his person and his historic mission. Thus in II Corinthians Paul compares, but in the form of a contrast, Christ to Moses, whose face was fleetingly illuminated by the glory of the vision on Sinai. He compares and contrasts the gospel with the old covenant, the meaning of which remains veiled to his readers, who are afraid of detaching themselves from it. He also compares the followers of Christ to those who turn from him and whose heart remains veiled: Christ 'is the image of God', he says, for the glory of God 'which is on his face' lightens the hearts of believers and illuminates for them the gospel of the glory of Christ (II Cor.4.3–6). The relationship established here between the image which is Christ and the 'light of glory' is a complex metaphor which shows that the light of revelation is in Christ to become the light of faith in us. Christ is the image of God, just as he is the one who truly reveals God, the one who lifts the veil on the truth of God and his salvation: that is what the gospel as a whole teaches us.

This answer calls for other explanations: Christ is the perfect revealer of God because God is present in him – but how does he make this presence *visible* so that we can say that he is God's image? We know the answer given by dogma: Christ is the perfect image of God because he is of the same nature as the Father, being his Son and his Word.[9] Certainly. But this true image, precisely because of its absolute perfection, is image only in the metaphorical sense: it is like God, who cannot take the place of an image for us. By definition the true image is as invisible as God himself. One could say that the divinity of Christ makes itself visible in his humanity – but how? Either by transparency, in which case we fall back into iconic theology (but the glory which makes itself visible belongs to the deity; it is not the image of another thing). Or by the transformation of his humanity which bears witness to the divine presence that inhabits it (but this humanity is reduced to the role of a mirror which reflects passively what takes place in it). It is not an image by its own nature and activity: that would be a theology of glory which did not do full justice to the humanity of Christ, since it would not leave it the freedom of being what it is or of becoming what it makes of itself. So one is 'reduced' to thinking that Christ is the image of God as man, in his own body, on the level of his historical existence – and that brings us back to the simple evidence of the Gospels.

When Jesus says 'he who has seen me has seen the Father' (John 14.9) – a particularly 'idolatrous' statement for pure monotheists – he is far from identifying himself with the Father or suggesting that he makes the Father visible in his flesh. On the contrary, he confronts people with the assurance that they would want to give themselves in order to keep God in view. However, he speaks to his companions of a natural and everyday vision: 'Have I been so long with you, Philip, and you do not know me!' He shows them that if, as they see him alive and hear him speak, they recognize him as one sent by God, who does and says the things of God in the power of the Spirit, they will not fail to know God's truth, namely by the visible bond which indissolubly unites Jesus to God as Son to Father. To see Jesus is to discern the presence of God in him. It is the sole means, but the authentic means, of seeing God. The Gospel agrees everywhere with the testimony that Jesus gives here: it is through human words – parables drawn from everyday life and human actions – among the poor and the sick, friends and enemies, that Jesus reveals to the simple the secret of God, namely that God forgives and he loves. It is by obeying his mission to the end and showing solidarity to the extreme with human suffering that Jesus reveals how far God humbles himself for us, to the point that, on seeing him die, the pagan centurion proclaims him Son of God (Mark 15.39). It is above all when we see God 'raise' him from the dead that we have a revelation of how God is Father both of Jesus and of all those whom he calls to take a place beside him. However, it is then also that Christ is recognized at the same time as Son of

God, the new Adam (I Cor.15.45–49), the first-fruits of a new race of human beings whose humanity is 'renewed in the image of its creator' (Col.3.10), and that explains in what way he is 'image of God'.

## III. Image rather than icon

If the image of God in human beings is restored in any way in its original beauty and, as far as the man Jesus is concerned, 'reflects as in a mirror the glory of the Lord' (II Cor.3.18), we must understand that Jesus is himself the image of God in a unique way, since it is through him that we are marked with the image which destines us to bear the likeness of the Son of God. However, he is also like us, since it is our own image that he has had to assume as his in order to fashion it in himself, in his own humanity, in the likeness of the divine original. Thus there is fulfilled in the course of history from the first to the last Adam a circuit which leads to Christ the image of the God who is present in the human being and then back in every human being to that which is in Christ. This is one and the same image, but bipolar: it is the history of human beings in solidarity with Christ or the solidarity of human beings with themselves with the world and with Christ in the same historicity.

So it is against this horizon of historicity that the question of the truth of the representations of God is decided. The true knowledge of God is accessible to us only through God's image of himself which he has put in us to make his truth visible to us. This image is not an innate character imprinted in our beings; it is a historical task to be fulfilled. It is not purely individual, but collective; it is the vocation of each and every one to realize human freedom in the fullness of responsibility for others and for the world, and doing so in 'walking before God', according to the biblical expression – God whose infinite freedom touches on ours by drawing it on, and whose countenance impresses its likeness in the humanity of which human beings write the history.

Christ is the perfect image of God because he has realized human freedom in himself in a total yes to God and others, to the point of totally dispossessing himself of self. He had the power to do this because he bore in himself the Word of life, the creative Word which is God's yes to his creation. He could do so effectively only because he assumed existence in the communal history of human beings. That is why he is the *image* rather than the *icon*. We do not have the pure uprising of the Eternal in time, which would reduce the world to nothingness, but the 'work' (John 14.10) of reshaping a historical heritage which makes the humanity of Christ the true revelation of the divinity of God in the image which has become visible in him of the 'humanity of God' – to use an expression of Karl Barth's which could not be suspected of 'idolatry'.

The sole aim of these reflections is to offer a prolegomena to a logical critique of the truth of theological discourse. Discourse which puts itself modestly but firmly in a cultural context, either a project for liberation or a political dimension, has more chance of verifying these premises than discourse which seeks to speak of the pure splendour of the deity, of the pure interiority of the soul's journey towards God, or the pure rigour of the divine order which is to reign in creation. In conclusion, I would retain those allusions which have no programmatic element: the carnal weight of the image is a more certain 'measure' of truth than the lightness of the icon.

*Translated by John Bowden*

## Notes

1.  For what follows see Jean-Luc Marion, *Dieu sans l'être*, Paris 1982, pp.15–37.
2.  Marion, ibid., p.28 n.14, bases his analysis on Pierre Chantraine, *Dictionnaire étymmologique de la langue grecque*, Paris 1968, p.254, 'who emphasizes that *eikô* primarily denotes the impression coming to the spectator from the thing itself as an authentic appearance'. I did not read anything of this kind in the 1990 edition with reference either to this verb (yield, draw back) or to *eoika*, p.354 (resemble, seem, imagine, invent, conjecture) or to *eikon* on p.355 (image, representation, comparison, affinity, resemblance).
3.  Marion, *Dieu sans l'être*, pp.29–30, refers to John of Damascus and Nicaea II (nn.15 and 16).
4.  These are the terms used by Olivier Clement, *Encyclopaedia Universalis* 11, 1990, 'Icône', p.884.
5.  L. Ouspensky, *Théologie de l'icône dans l'Église orthodoxe*, Paris 1980. In what follows I refer especially to pp.133–75.
6.  Ibid., pp.134–35, 151–53, 164–65 (where these two pictures are reproduced), 466–69 (Catholic art subscribes to human autonomy), 471 ('Raphael subjected the natural vision of the human eye to the control of his autonomous reason and by doing so distanced himself from this vision').
7.  Ouspensky, *Théologie de l'icône*, p.211, referring to the teaching of Gregory Palamas, explains that the 'light of Tabor' is the manifestation of the 'divine energy' which is a mode of God's existence, as distinct from his essence, 'a presence of the Uncreated in the created . . . really revealed and contemplated by the saints as a divine glory and an ineffable beauty'.

8. Ouspensky largely takes his doctrine of the icon from Hesychasm, to which he devotes several chapters of his book: a theology of monks, who were often responsible for the art of the icon.
9. It would be unwise to presuppose these concepts where Christ is called the image of God, for example in Col. 1.15 interpreted by means of other texts where an allusion to his 'pre-existence' can be suspected, like Phil. 2.6; Heb. 1.3 or John 1.18. However, I shall not enter into this discussion.

# The Relevance of Negative Theology

HERMANN HÄRING

## I. Does God really become human?

Thirty-three years ago, Ernst Bloch, the great atheist of late Marxism, sub-
scribed with great emphasis to the Christian statement of faith that God has
become man in Jesus, and that therefore Jesus is of the same substance as
God. It was important to him, as it was to the orthodoxy of the early church,
that the famous iota should remain banned from this statement of faith:
Jesus is not only of a similar substance (*homoi-ousios*) but of the same substance (*homo-ousios*) as God. For in this way God finally leaves his divine
heights, and heaven is 'transformed into a city of men', so that the 'Christ
impulse can live, even if God is dead'.[1] Some pious readers felt supported by
these orthodox words and found only the last clause about the dead God
somewhat enigmatic. However, here they had not understood Bloch, since
in fact Bloch did not want to confirm belief in God but finally to establish
human beings in their comprehensive rights, freed from God. So Bloch was
proud of discovering this 'atheism in Christianity'. According to his com-
pelling logic, if God has become man, then God has given up his divinity.
God is no longer God, for how could that which is divine at the same time be
human? Therefore for him the double statement of the Council of
Chalcedon – Jesus is at the same time of both divine and human nature; is at
the same time God and of the same substance as us – is contradictory
sophism.

Of course no believer will go along with Bloch's argument, but it deeply
unsettles all those who accept the traditional picture of the incarnation of
God as an objective description. Anyone who imagines the incarnation as a
transformation in which 'God' becomes 'man' has overlooked the mystery
and the paradox that we have here. How can God appear in human form, and
how can we discover the presence of God in a particular human being?[2]
When, for example, the Johannine prologue claims that the Word has
become flesh (John 1.14), and when, for example, Jesus says in the judgment

discourse, 'What you have done for the least of my brothers and sisters you have done for me' (Matt. 25.40), every attempt at a descriptive, logically coherent image of God is shattered. Manifestly God cannot be tied to a limited identity. On the contrary, everything and nothing stand side by side; the light is at the same time darkness; the height becomes the abyss, and the near and the far cross. Where we expect salvation, we are hurled in to the diversity and terror of the human. Moreover because God, to use Paul Tillich's words, is only a symbol for 'God',[3] neither the most precise nor the most pious theology can tell us who or what 'God' really is.

Is that the basic statement of 'negative theology'? Did it not always begin from the fact that God is 'the ineffable mystery'? Indeed the core of any negative theology begins with this paradox which always finds God in what God is not, and which therefore knows that we cannot find God where human projections expect him. But if we are really shown that God encounters us in human beings and the world, then God has abandoned his own, self-contained identity. Then the quest for the 'ineffable mystery' – i.e. for the divine in God – is always bound up with waiting and disappointment, with uncertainty or ecstasy. The quest for God can become dangerous and has already driven many people mad; with good reason in the biblical tradition the desert became the classic place for encountering God.[4] For far too long 'negative theology' became only one (particularly pious or élitist) special form of Christian theology, perhaps as a limit case of mystical discourse about God, perhaps understood as filling the gaps in rational reflection. In reality, any theology worthy of the name begins with a basic discovery which blows open any rational logic[5] and which is expressed very precisely in the symbol of the incarnation of God. So the question should not be a merely technical one: how and at what points is negative theology reporting back today? From the religious starting point the question should be: how and through what experiences is theology today again reminded of its indispensable basis? If I see things rightly, this basic experience of the ineffable and the alien is making a comeback in the present situation at four points at the same time. We have:

- within *faith* and religion the experience of a God who keeps withdrawing himself;
- under the influence of *science* and technology symbols and codes in which 'God' become superfluous or is imperceptibly volatilized;
- in Western *culture* an understanding of reality in which the question of 'God' has no place;

- in our present-day *societies,* conditions which indicate more of God's impotence than of God's goodness.

At all these levels today a theology is called for which is confronted more with failure and the remoteness of God than with God's success and ultimate power. These questions are posed not only in the forum of the church but also in the forum of a society which is technologically orientated, which has a pluralistic world-view and which will not be content with the predominant injustice.

## II. The quest for the remote God

### *1. The remoteness of God in religion*

God is greater than our knowledge; according to the biblical and Christian tradition he is always already an ineffable God.[6] Yahweh's enigmatic naming of himself at the burning bush was always translated down the centuries in a lively way as 'I am who I am' (Ex. 3.14). It is echoed in the name which Jesus gives himself in the Gospel of John: 'I am the Way, the Truth and the Life' (John 14.6). Those who ask never learn who this Yahweh and who this Messiah really are; at the same time they know everything. They know that all desire and all hope has gone into these figures – and yet they stand with empty hands. God himself shows himself only by naming himself – in an unfathomable statement of himself – as 'God', as saviour or Messiah.[7]

Comparable experiences entered the tradition of the piety of the early church from Greek Platonism and from Hellenistic Gnosticism. According to Plotinus, God himself appears only as 'silence' and the inexpressible,[8] which cannot even communicate itself directly. Augustine gives a classic description of it in the mystical rapture which he experienced with his mother Monica in Ostia.[9] In a heartbeat of exaltation they experience a silence which transcends all sensual expressions and sounds; in an ineffable moment everything is communicated to the two of them. It is an experience in what cannot be experienced, an encounter of God in pure withdrawal, a sphere which thus evades any positive experience and any grasp. For Monica it finally means death. The theological tradition has translated this relationship of tension down the centuries into three epistemological stages and thus robbed it of its drama. The three stages are: all experience of God begins with a positive content; it can be named and analysed. So whoever experiences God first of all has to know and to report. This is the 'way of affirmation' (*via affirmationis*). But here a problem begins, for none of this content is adequate for God. It all falls short. So precisely because the state-ments are to apply to God, they have to be contradicted: this is the 'way of negation' (*via negationis*).

The third step is by no means a matter of course, nor can it be compelled, nor does it simply overcome the problem of the second stage. But in the incessant play of affirmation and negation, experience and knowledge are driven beyond themselves in a kind of mental and experiential trans-cendence. This has been called the way of 'ascending comparison' (*via eminentiae*).[10] This model has often been misunderstood or wrongly applied. The drama of Yes and No (which often meant of happiness and desperation) was degraded into a logical rule. Talk of God was no longer driven on, but domesticated. It was forgotten that we could not know God by way of logic or metaphysics.[11] It would in fact have been necessary to close one's eyes with the utmost concentration, at the same time to work out the encounter with God and allow oneself to be helped to surpass the way of logical argu-ment by that of illumination.

Negative theology is not specific to the Bible or indeed to Christianity. Rather, comparisons with the mystical schools of India, with Buddhism and Islam, make it clear that we have regularly domesticated and suppressed the danger of the negative experience of God. Moreover, negative theology in the traditional meaning of the word has become topical: talk of the God who surpasses all understanding is to be found everywhere. Here many people are breaking out of the religious conventions that they have learned and making images of God which no longer stand up to their everyday thought and practice. The critique of religion and hermeneutical thinking had already prepared the ground for this by interlocking images of God and images of human beings. God is manifestly present in reality only where his ineffable nature silences our voices. This is a critique of God for the sake of the true God. Presumably that is also why today many images of God with-in the churches are also being shattered and many people in Western cultures, even believers, feel attracted to amorphous images of God and to a new kind of religion. The distance from the clear God who is at our disposal has grown, as has the conviction that trust in the true and all-embracing God transcends the doctrines and rules of the churches. In secularized societies in particular the call of a new spirituality has become a loud one; the Netherlands has now become a prime example of this new sense of religion.[12] In this development, of course, voluntary ideologies and a faith which is ready for risks, the trivialization of feeling and the experience of abysses, lie side by side. However, the new tendency towards a deeper faith is un-mistakable: theology and the church have an important task of clarification here. Against the background of negative theology, the crisis of God in the West becomes a unique opportunity for renewal.

## 2. *Farewell to language*

For centuries, 'God' was completely at home in Western culture. That has changed. With his cry 'God is dead! . . . We have killed him!' Nietzsche was primarily referring to the culture of his time.[13] Today it is clearer than ever that even unprejudiced people speak of God in Western culture only with misunderstandings and incomprehension. What is the explanation of that?

I shall not repeat the classic theories of secularization here under the well-known headings of the differentiation, rationalization, democratization or secularization of our society. According to more recent studies, it does not follow from them that religion has disappeared or withdrawn to a private sphere.[14] Evidently the processes are more complex than that. Here I shall limit myself to the imperceptible change in the world of symbols, to the inner shifts in words and concepts which formerly referred as a matter of course to God and transcendence. Such shifts take place imperceptibly and unconsciously. And the fields of reference in which a religious language can develop and have an effect are changing just as unconsciously and in a way beyond our control. Our talk of God bears the strong stamp of a feudal and agricultural society, of an experience of existence which was heavily dependent on questions of nature and primary needs. In this experience, God appeared as father (or mother) and lord, as protector against the forces of nature and the guardian of salvation, as a helper in sickness and an experi-ence of guilt – an experience on which no educationalist or psychologist had yet reflected. God was the one who could create and preserve directly the freedom of the children of God. People called on God in sickness and famine, in war and great catastrophes. Experiences of democracy and scien-tific success, developments in technology and a life accepting responsibility for oneself have not yet entered religious language. Of course we still expect God's protection and still hope for God's forgiveness. I am not claiming that the 'old' symbols are simply out of date or have become ineffective. But they are no longer taken for granted. They have at least become ambivalent, and speak not only of divine but also of human power. Modern societies have developed comprehensive scientific and technological systems which take on (quasi-) divine functions. One might think of the systems of education and food supply, of health and communication, of insurance and transport; and of the global and even orbital dimensions that our technological activity has achieved. We human beings are now concerned about being adult and having freedom; we want boundless energy and inner stability. A modern hospital cares for every organ and can even implant organs in living bodies; machines take over the heartbeat and can prolong life at will. And machines can take one to other continents in a matter of hours. Doctors and technicians have now gained incomparably more knowledge than former generations ever expected from God: alongside the libraries of the world, the wisdom of the Bible shrinks into a modest building block of a few texts. The expectations of, for example, contemporary gene technology are boundless. The fascination with all that we can do, the utility of all our achievements, also benefits believers.

What has happened? What was formerly reserved for God has now created its own secular instruments. Of course the limits and risks, birth and death, broken relationships and burdensome guilt have not been done away with, but in the face of nuclear power, gene technology and the modern technology of war, they have been moved to the limits of our everyday actions. That is reason enough for often defending belief apologetically or ironically: 'God is dead,' I hear friends say, 'and technology is his corpse.' But this 'corpse' is our life. We all take it for granted that we live in these new spheres of expectations and fulfilments; eschatology is perfected in the genetic laboratory. So technology has attracted to itself the fascination of religious symbols.[15] Even the apocalyptic end has today been handed over to human beings, and we can meditate on the power of the atom.[16] So God is secretly departing from the worlds of our immediate expectations and imagination, or at least he is being given formidable competition: the process goes one stage further with every generation. We are lapsing into a general ignorance about religions, not only because their content has become uninteresting but because religious language, the symbol 'God', is losing its irreplaceable power to provide orientation. It is drying out.

But have not theologians and linguistic scholars been reacting to this for decades? Have we not been studying Wittgenstein and Ricoeur, Schillebeeckx and Tracy very precisely for a long time? Our theology contains a high degree of hermeneutical and linguistic reflection, and pastoral theology draws the consequences of that. We know the possibilities and the random nature of language: we know about the religious 'language game' and about the significance of myth and narrative for our religious identity. It is precisely there that the danger lies, for the more reflection there is behind our talk, the more it disrupts our immediacy to God. God is bidding farewell to our language-world because we experience this as a linguistic and not as a religious problem.

At this point a new negative theology is called for in the framework of a theology of culture. Such a theology must understand the three stages of statement, negation and transcending as a cultural problem. Those who only reinterpret and explain the old symbols have not yet understood the sub-terranean shifts and loss of orientation which have taken place in religious language. Therefore it is a matter of learning outside specifically religious language, from what concerns human beings: from poetry and literature,[17] the graphic arts and the great secular visionaries of our time. We must succeed in going back behind the explicit religious forms to the forms of a primary and elementary, perhaps invisible, religion.[18] I call the negative theology which withstands this process of reduction to basic elements a provisional or temporary theology. Real negative theology begins with the discovery that this loss of God coincides with the loss of humanity, with a general weariness. According to J.-P. Wils, technological culture is not only entangled in its own body but is increasingly also leading a 'prothesis existence on the machine'; all that is left of us is a 'naked' existence. Perhaps God can be found again where there is again a quest for truth in protest against injustice and in the cry of pain.[19] The God of this farewell is report-ing back at most in many unexpected places, under the signs of his opposite.

## 3. Exodus from reality

A third place where God is denied is closely connected with this, and it is here that questions about God unexpectedly accumulate, and not from the theological side. This problem place was also noted by the critics of religion earlier than it was noted by theologians. Heidegger already pointed out that in theology 'God' had been degraded to a thing, to an object. He spoke of 'onto-theology'. Later he 'crossed through' the basic word being, i.e. put a cross through it, to make it clear that it was close to being interchangeable with nothingness. I cannot describe the debate about constructivism here. Often it is rightly presented as a form of the critique of religion. The 'God' for whom we are excessively concerned contradicts himself; for he precedes all language, is wholly other, and thus is the only word that may not (yet) be named.[20] Or God is, quite simply, the wholly Other of whom at most we per-ceive a trace.[21] So the critique of religion is focussed on the use of the word 'God'. The critique is not new. As early as 1925 Bultmann put the question,

'What sense does it make to talk of God?' His reply was that we can speak of God only 'when we must'.[22] But why has this situation become more acute today? Why can we now experience the presence of God only in silence?[23]

The literary critic George Steiner has added an important aspect to the answer. In his view the culture of the West has abrogated the treaty between word and reality: that is why a farewell has also been said to God.[24] With language our talk of 'God' also becomes void of content: at most it is a random container for the positive or negative experiences that someone collects. One could talk of an 'epistemological atheism'.[25] Only now does theology arrive at a No beyond which it is hardly possible to go. It has no positive point of contact: for the first time it begins with a No which no longer even recalls God, and therefore does not even regret God's absence. But the reason for this does not simply lie in the fact that 'God' is in any case an incomprehensible word which we do better to surround with silence than with chatter. The reason is that – in language and in practice – we have modelled the image of a technological reality which is at our disposal. Reality no longer offers any secret, nor does it any longer offer any beauty; we are no longer immersed in it, and no longer participate in it as in a vital element of life. What has to be changed? We must attempt to stop despising and dominating material reality and deal with it only respectfully and honestly, in a 'courteous way'. That is a matter of aesthetics – as a protest against the reification that there is in strategies of subjection. We certainly cannot recall 'God' to a flat present, and it is good that we cannot; as Lévinas says, God must remain attainable to us only in traces. We have rightly learned this in the age of the critique of religion. So in our culture, theology needs a 'hermeneutics of absence'[26] which does not exert any compulsion, but leaves the Other (God included) in his freedom and his distance. So it must be possible to speak with respect and dignity about God in such a way that while this ineffable mystery is mentioned and addressed, it is neither imposed on the world nor dissected, for what we keep silent about is left to inarticulated feelings. But how can we get to that from the starting point of radical negativity? Evidently in this remoteness of God for non-believers, too, there is a remnant which can hardly be described, but is left unresolved. There remain – however concealed and indirect – the questions of reality and meaning, of birth and death, of my self and our selves. It is a matter of respect and autonomy, a pre-religious 'Where do the questions come from'?[27] Faith in God today must have such small and elementary beginnings.

However, there is a danger in this undertaking. This enthusiastic search corresponds to an egocentric society which is incapable of controlling others. It would be a pity to use the term negative theology for such a quest, which in the end costs nothing. What I am referring to here is the impatience of those who – behind the mask of all their needs – again discover a last desire and attempt to drink from their own wells, which are full of rubble.[28] That brings them into the sharpest contradiction with a society which they experience as the wilderness. Their quest does not allow them to create a religious excuse for themselves. So, as I shall attempt to demonstrate, resistance is also necessary. Without the context of action, even a negative theology fed by mysticism does not make sense.

## III. Changing society

In retrospect, the twentieth century presents itself as an era of catastrophes and indescribable cruelty. The dominant cultures have made themselves instruments of tremendous power. None of the global vicious circles of poverty, oppression, racism and sexism has been broken through. News of one catastrophe comes hot on the heels of another. It is finally time to confront the negative theologies with this misery. So I shall only repeat what is already known. Anyone who according to the Bible and early Christianity 'knows' God is not performing an isolated rational act but entering into an experienced relationship to God and the world. It makes sense to talk of the knowledge of God or of silence only if these actions are embedded in concrete life. The emancipatory theologies of the twentieth century have rediscovered the old dimension of this praxis which is common to all humankind, and at the same time is social. Here the problem of theodicy proves to be a question to our human action. Whereas formerly theodicy was meant to stabilize religion, now it discloses its dangerous potential.[29] Auschwitz became an outcry, the great question about whether God is good or impotent. Soon after that, liberation theology demonstrated to the classical theologies of the West that it did not have to accept the absence of God as an abstract fate. It is not a matter of pious interpretation but of a consistent changing of reality.

Thus it is proving in the practical sphere that affirmation, negation and intensification are fused together. They have now become trust in God, fury and protest against God, and action in solidarity for a better future. Ten years ago E.Borgman made an interesting attempt to interpret the theologies of emancipation (liberation theology, black theologies and feminist theology), in the light of their impulse towards praxis, as negative theologies. His starting point was that Christian faith expresses the liberating God. This is a God who has seen the misery of his people and is leading it to freedom (Ex. 3.7–8). The terrifying discovery of Christian theologians is therefore that reality itself, the processes of exploitation and oppression, contradict this talk of the liberating God. So it is not just a universal experience of divine truth that is at work in the theologies of emancipation. There are not 'traces' of God in God's creation – pre-industrial and quite archaic; rather – in a concrete and post-atheistic situation – there are what Schillebeeckx calls 'experiences of contrast' which are embedded in movements of protest and opposition and which at the same time strive for a better future. Our societies are stamped by traces of the anti-godly; by our actions these are to be countered by the traces of God. These new traces begin as human actions. The cry of the poor and the tortured, the indignation of women and the weeping of children, can be turned into a better future. We can help one another; here the statement about the incarnation of God takes on concrete meaning.

It could be objected that this situation is not new, for former generations too were not content with this world and therefore set all their hopes on another world to come. But it is precisely here that the critical point lies. Just as the former standard theology thought that one could overcome the negations in the knowledge of God once and for all, so too it did not endure the injustice of this world but suppressed it. By contrast, an emancipatory praxis of faith – like that of Job – also disputes with God if need be, because it is fighting for a better reality. God has been done away with in the world not because of some process of secularization but because of the blatant injustice in the world. Because God appears in human faces, we are the ones who disfigure God's face, and God remains in a new way a disputed mystery, for only from human beings can we learn what God's faithfulness and solidarity is about. We do not act as a substitute for religion, but as a test case of authentic religion.

## Conclusion

I began with the question 'Does God really become human?' I then made it clear how this incarnation changes faith in God. God confronts us with abysses and changes in culture: God is never himself, never appears as a monopoly but – especially in a fragmented culture – in fragments.[30] God even allows himself to be displaced from our world, and confronts us with a reality from which God has been removed. Does not such an image of God end up in hopeless randomness? Would we not have been left with more certainty, orientation and more 'positive' theology if God had simply remained God? I do not know. All I know is this: Christians on their way are offered the history of Jesus as a matrix of successful incarnation. In the history of Jesus, negative theology became concrete as hostility and repudiation, as confrontation with institutions that would not learn, as suffering and death, as abandonment by God and fellow human beings. Our histories are no different from this, and yet they are quite different. Therefore every generation writes its own negative theology. If in the Christian tradition Jesus Christ is said to be 'of the same substance as God and human beings', this is not because he walks over this earth as a divine figure, but only because we can attempt to do what is decisive in memory of him. We can discover God's face in the life and fate of the humiliated, and see that the incarnation of God becomes effective and public. That does not spare us any toil, but it does nurture the certainty that God will wipe away all tears if we give him the hands to do so.

*Translated by John Bowden*

## Notes

1. E. Bloch, *Atheismus im Christentum*, Hamburg 1986, ch.5, no.33, last paragraph.
2. The concern of the christologies 'from below' as developed e.g. by L. Boff, H. Küng and E. Schillebeeckx in the 1970s was to clarify this.
3. P. Tillich, *Dynamics of Faith*, World Perspectives, Series X, New York 1957, ch. III.
4. The contemporary philosopher P. Sloterdijk, *Weltfremdheit*, Frankfurt 1993, pp.80–117, gives an unexpectedly positive evaluation of the early Christian desert spirituality ('Where are the monks going? The dialectic of flight from the world and the quest for the world').
5. I shall not investigate here very strong forms of expression of a negative (mystical or aphophatic) theology of other religions, for example in Judaism, Islam or Buddhism.
6. M. C. Srajek, *In the Margins of Deconstruction. Jewish Conceptions of Ethics in Emmanuel Lévinas and Jacques Derrida*, Pittsburgh 2000.
7. P. Chatelion Counet, *De sarcofaag van het Woord. Postmoderniteit, deconstructie en het Johannesevangelie*, Kampen 1995, pp.225–51.
8. D. Carabine, *The Unknown God: Negative Theology: The Platonic Tradition, Plato to Eriugena*, New York 1995.
9. *Confessions*, Book IX, 10.23–26.

10. Thus recently the expert J. Hochstaffl, 'Negative Theologie', *LThK³*, Vol.7, 1998, 723–25.

11. D. R. Law, *Hiddenness of God: Negative Theology in the Pseudonymous Works of Kierkegaard*, Oxford 1993.

12. A. van Harskamp, *Het nieuw-religieuze verlangen*, Kampen 2000.

13. U. Willers, *Friedrich Nietzsches antichristliche Christologie. Eine Theologische Rekonstruktion*, Vienna 1988.

14. J. Casanova, *Public Religions in the Modern World*, Chicago 1994; van Harskamp, *Het nieuw-religieuze verlangen* (n.12), pp.23–24.

15. There is a very impressive discussion of this development in D. Koelega and W. Drees (eds), *God & Co? Geloven in een technologische cultur*, Kampen 2000; for the quotation about God's corpse see F. de Lange, 'De "dood van God" en de techniek', ibid., pp.71–92.

16. P.Sloterdijk, *Kritik der zynischen Vernunft* I, Frankfurt 1983, pp.256–61: meditation on bombs.

17. K.-J. Kuschel, *The Poet as Mirror. Human Nature, God and Jesus in Twentieth-Century Literature*, London 1999.

18. J. Assmann, *Herrschaft und Heil. Politische Theologie in Altägypten, Israel und Europa*, Munich 2000, pp.40–42; T.Luckmann. *Die unsichtbare Religion*, Frankfurt 1991.

19. J.-P. Wils, *Die gross Erschöpfung. Kulturethische Probleme vor der Jahrtausendwende*, Paderborn 1994; see also *Concilium* 1999/4, *Faith in a Society of Instant Gratification*.

20. J. Derrida, 'Comment ne pas parler', in id., *Psyché. Inventions de l'autre*, Paris 1989, pp.535–95.

21. E. Lévinas, *Die Spur des Anderen, Untersuchungen zur Phänomenologie und Sozialphilosophie*, Freiburg and Munich, 3rd edn 1992.

22. R. Bultmann, 'What Sense Does it Make to Talk of God?', *Faith and Understanding*, London and New York 1969, pp.26–37.

23. P. Chatelion Counet, *Over God zwijgen. Postmodernbijbellezen*, Zoetermeer 1998.

24. G. Steiner, *Real Presences*, London 1989.

25. *Atheistisch manifest. Drie wijsgerige opstellen over godsdienst en moraal*, Amsterdam 1995.

26. J. P. Wils, 'Die Gegenwart des Mythos? Überlegungen zu einer theologischen Ästhetik der Abwesenheit' in W. Lesch (ed), *Theologie und ästhetische Erfahrung. Beiträge zur Begegnung von Religion und Kunst*, Darmstadt 1994, pp.166–82.

27. W. Weischedel, *Der Gott der Philosophen* II, Darmstadt 1975, pp.206–18.

28. G. Gutiérrez, *We Drink from Our Own Wells*, Maryknoll and London 1984; cf. J. Van Nieuwenhove, *Bronnen van de bevrijding. Variante in de theologie van Gustavo Gutiérrez*, Kampen 1991.

29. H. Häring, *Das Böse in der Welt. Gottes Macht oder Ohnmacht?*, Darmstadt 1999, pp.128–71.

30. J. Pohier,*God in Fragments*, London 1985; J. Miles, *God. A Biography*, New York 1995.

# Contributors

DAVID N. POWER was born in Dublin in 1932 and is currently Professor Emeritus at The Catholic University of America, Washington DC, USA. He has taught theology and liturgy in Ireland, Rome and Washington and was for some twenty years a member of the general editorial board of *Concilium*. His latest book is *Sacrament: the Language of God's Giving*, New York: Crossroad 1999.

Address: 391 Michigan Avenue, NE, Washington DC 20017, USA

MARY GREY was formerly Professor of Feminism in Christendom at the Catholic University of Nijmegen, the Netherlands, and then Professor of Contemporary Theology at the University of Southampton, Great Britain. She is now working at Sarum College, Salisbury, as Scholar-in-Residence, and as Professor of Theology at the University of Wales, at Lampeter. With her husband Nicholas she is involved in an NGO, *Wells for India,* active in the desert of Rajasthan, north-west India.

Address: Sarum College, 19 The Close, Salisbury, Wiltshire SP1 2EE, UK

MARCELLA ALTHAUS-REID is an Argentinian Materialist theologian. She is director of a MTh course in Theology, Culture and Development and a lecturer in Christian Ethics and Systematic Theology in the University of Edinburgh, Scotland. She obtained her Bachelor in Theology from ISEDET, Buenos Aires, and her PhD from St Andrews University, Scotland. Prior to studying for her doctorate she was co-ordinator of a Freirean conscientization process in deprived areas of Dundee and Perth. She is a Quaker. Dr Althaus-Reid is a member of the Association of European Women in Theological Research and is on the Feminist Advisory Board for *Concilium*. She is author of *Indecent Theology. Theological Perversions on Sex, Gender and Politics*, London: Routledge 2000, and her numerous other publications include 'On using Skirts without Underwear. Indecent Theology contesting the Liberation Theology of the Pueblo: Poor Women contesting Christ' in *Feminist Theology*, 20 January 1999, pp.39–51; 'Hermeneutics of Transgression. Time and the Children of the Street in Buenos Aires' in G. de Schrijver (ed), *Liberation Theologies on Shifting Grounds*, Leuven University Press 1998; and 'Doing a Theology of the Memory' in M. Best and P. Hussey, *Life out of Death. The Feminine Spirit of El Salvador*, London: CIIR 1996.

Address: Faculty of Divinity, New College, The University of Edinburgh, Mound Place, Edinburgh EH1 2LX, Scotland.

OLA SIGURDSON is Associate Professor in the Department of Theology and Religious Studies at the University of Lund, Sweden.

Address: Angemarken 1, S-413 20 Gothenburg, Sweden.
e-mail: ola.Sigurdson@tripnet.se        voice: + 46 31 201616

CHRISTOPH THEOBALD was born in Cologne in 1946 and became a Jesuit in the Province of France in 1978. He is Professor of Fundamental and Dogmatic Theology in the Theological Faculty of the Centre Sèvres, Paris, and editor of *Recherches de Science Religieuse*, to which he contributes a bulletin on systematic theology (God - Trinity). His works in the history of modern theology and systematic theology include *Maurice Blondel und das Problem der Modernität. Beitrag zu einer epistemologischen Standortbestimmung zeitgenössischer Fundamentaltheologie*, Frankfurt 1988; 'De Vatican I aux années 1950' and 'Le concile Vatican II et ses suites' in *Histoire des dogmes* 4, Paris 1996; 'Le devenir de la théologie catholique depuis Vatican II', *Histoire du christianisme* 13, Paris 2000, and, with Philippe Charru, *La Pensée musicale de Jean-Sébastian Bach. Les chorals du Catéchisme luthérien dans la 'Clavier-Ubung' (III)*, Paris 1993.

Address; 15, rue Monsieur, 75007 Paris, France.

NONNA VERNA HARRISON has degrees from Yale, Oxford, and the Graduate Theological Union in Berkeley, California. She has taught at St Vladimir's Orthodox Theological Seminary, is currently a Visiting Lecturer at the Institute for Orthodox Christian Studies in Cambridge, England, and lives in Berkeley. She is the author of *Grace and Human Freedom according to S. Gregory of Nyssa*, as well as of many scholarly articles on topics in patristics and Orthodox theology.

Address: 1944 Curtis Street, Apt. 16, Berkely CA 94702, USA
e-mail: SrNonna@aol.com

MARK O'BRIEN was born in 1945 in Wagga Wagga, New South Wales, Australia. He holds the degrees of Bachelor of Science (BSc) (University of New England, Australia), Sacrae Theologiae Baccalaureatus (STB) (Universita San Tommaso, Rome but obtained through St Mary's House of Studies, Tallaght, Ireland), License in Sacred Scripture (LSS) (Pontifical Biblical Institute, Rome), Doctor of Theology (D.Theol) (Melbourne College of Divinity). He has held the positions of Lecturer in Old Testament Studies at Yarra Theological Union, Melbourne (a campus of the Melbourne College of Divinity) (1977–1992); Academic Dean of Yarra Theological Union (1990–1992); Provincial of the Province of the Assumption, Dominican Friars (1993–2000). His publications include *The Deuteronomistic History Hypothesis* (OBO 920), Gottingen: Vandenhoeck & Ruprecht 1989; and, all with Antony F. Campbell, *Sources of the Pentateuch: Texts, Introductions, Annotations*, Minneapolis: Fortress Press 1993; entries on '1–2 Samuel' and '1–2 Kings in *The International Bible Commentary*, The Liturgical Press 1999; *Unfolding the Deuteronomistic History: Origins, Upgrades, Present Text*, Fortress Press, forthcoming.

Address: S. Dominic's Priory, 816 Riversdale Road, Camberwell, Victoria 3124, Australia.

SEÁN FREYNE is a member of the editorial board of *Concilium* and is Professor of Theology at Trinity College, Dublin. His biblical studies have been conducted at the Pontifical Biblical Institute, Rome, and Jerusalem, and at the Institute for Ancient Judaism of the University of Tübingen. He is the author of several books and many articles on various biblical topics. His research interests deal especially with the social and religious world of Galilee in the Second Temple period.

Address: 24, Charleville Road, Dublin 6, Ireland.

CLAUDE GEFFRÉ was born in Niort and joined the Dominicans of the French Province in 1948. He was Professor and Rector of the Dominican Faculties at Le Saulchoir between 1957 and 1968 and then Professor of Fundamental Theology at the Theological Faculty of the Catholic Institut in Paris from 1968 to 1996. From then until 1999 he was director of the École Biblique in Jerusalem. He was a member of the Editorial Committee of *Concilium* from 1965 to 1994. His publications include *Un nouvel âge de la théologie*, 1972; *Le christianisme au risque de l'interprétation*, 1983; *Passion de l'homme, passion de Dieu,* 1991; *Profession théologien. Quelle pensée chrétienne pour le XXIe siècle?*, 1999.

Address : 143, Boulevard Raspail, 75007 Paris, France.
e-mail : clgeffre@free.fr

ELAINE WAINWRIGHT lectures in Biblical Studies and Feminist Theology in the Brisbane College of Theology and is a faculty member of the Catholic Theological College in that consortium. She is also Visiting Fellow in the School of Theology at Griffith University. Her most recent publication is *Shall We Look for Another: A Feminist Rereading of the Matthean Jesus*. She teaches and publishes both nationally and internationally.

Address: Catholic Theological College, Approach Road, Banyo, Queensland 4014, Australia.
e-mail: E.Wainwright@mailbox.gu.edu.au

CHRISTOPH SCHWÖBEL was born 1955 and is currently Professor of Systematic Theology (Dogmatics and Ecumenical Theology) and Director of the Ecumenical Institute at the University of Heidelberg. Previously he taught Systematic Theology at the University of Kiel and at King's College London (University of London).

Address: Ökumenisches Institut Universität Heidelberg, Plankengasse1, D-69117 Heidelberg, Germany.
e-mail: Cschwoebel@t-online.de

WERNER G. JEANROND was born in Saarbrücken in 1955 and studied theology, literature and philosophy at the Universities of Saarbrücken,

Regensburg and Chicago. From 1981 to 1994 he was Lecturer in Systematic Theology and Fellow of Trinity College, University of Dublin. Since 1994 he has been Professor of Systematic Theology at the University of Lund in Sweden. His publications include *Text and Interpretation as Categories of Theological Thinking* (1988, German 1986); *Theological Hermeneutics* (1991, 1994, Italian 1994, French 1995, Polish 1999); *Call and Response: The Challenge of Christian Life* (1995, Swedish 1996, German 1999); *Guds Närvaro* (1998).

Address: Faculty of Theology, Lund University, Allhelgona Kyrkogata 8, SE-223 62 Lund, Sweden.

JOSEPH MOINGT was born in 1915 and became a Jesuit in 1939. He was Professor of Systematic Theology successively at the Jesuit Faculty of Lyons-Fourvière and then at the Catholic Institute of Paris, and now holds that post at the Jesuit Faculty of the Sèvres Centre in Paris. He has been editor of *Recherches de Science religieuse* since 1968. His most recent book is *L'homme qui venait de Dieu*, Paris 1993.

Address: 15 rue Monsieur, 75007 Paris, France.

HERMANN HÄRING was born in 1937 and studied theology in Münich and Tübingen; between 1969 and 1980 he worked at the Institute of Ecumenical Research in Tübingen; since 1980 he has been Professor of Dogmatic Theology at the Catholic University of Nijmegen. His books include *Kirche und Kerygma. Das Kirchenbild in der Buitmannschule*, 1972; *Die Macht des Bösen. Das Erbe Augustins*, 1979; *Zum Problem des Bösen in der Theologie*, 1985; *Hans Küng. Breaking Through*, London 1998; *Das Böse in der Welt*, 1999. He was co-editor of the *Wörterbuch des Christentums*, 1988, and has written articles on ecelesiology and christology, notably for *Tijdschrift voor Theologie*.

Address: Katholicke Universitcit, Faculteit der Godgeleerdheit, Erasmusgebouw, Erasmusplein 1, 6525 HT Nijmegen, Netherlands.

# CONCILIUM

# Concilium Subscription Information

*Issues to be published in 2001*

| February | 2001/1: *God: Experience and Mystery*<br>edited by Werner Jeanrond and Christoph Theobald |
| :--- | :--- |
| April | 2001/2: *The Return of the Just War*<br>edited by María Pilar Aquino Vargas and Dietmar Mieth |
| June | 2001/3: *The Oecumenical Constitution of Churches*<br>edited by Oscar Beozzo and Giuseppe Ruggieri |
| October | 2001/4: *Islamophobia*<br>edited by Elisabeth Schüssler Fiorenza and Karl-Josef Kuschel |
| December | 2001/5: *Globalization and its Victims*<br>edited by Jon Sobrino and Felix Wilfred |